The Heart of the Mission

THE HEART
of the
MISSION

SIMPLE WAYS
to Bring People
to JESUS

Cande de Leon

Our Sunday Visitor
Huntington, Indiana

Nihil Obstat
Msgr. Michael Heintz, Ph.D.
Censor Librorum

Imprimatur
✠ Kevin C. Rhoades
Bishop of Fort Wayne-South Bend
August 21, 2020

The *Nihil Obstat* and *Imprimatur* are official declarations that a book is free from doctrinal or moral error. It is not implied that those who have granted the *Nihil Obstat* and *Imprimatur* agree with the contents, opinions, or statements expressed.

Our Sunday Visitor Publishing Division
Our Sunday Visitor, Inc.
200 Noll Plaza
Huntington, IN 46750
www.osv.com
1-800-348-2440

ISBN: 978-1-68192-664-3 (Inventory No. T2532)
1. RELIGION—Christian Ministry—Evangelism.
2. RELIGION—Christian Ministry—General.
3. RELIGION—Christianity—Catholic.

eISBN: 978-1-68192-665-0
LCCN: 2020944350

Cover design: Amanda Falk
Cover art: AdobeStock
Interior design: Amanda Falk

PRINTED IN THE UNITED STATES OF AMERICA

Dedicated to Rosemary, Isabella, Abigail, Alexandra, and Sophia de Leon.

May God give you wisdom as you work to advance His mission.

I love you.

CONTENTS

INTRODUCTION

If you've picked up this book, I'm guessing you're looking for a way to engage with your Catholic faith in a deeper way. Maybe, like me, you've been Catholic all your life; or maybe you're new to the Faith and looking for ways to be more involved in the Church's mission. Maybe you aren't quite sure what it actually means to be Catholic and how your faith can have an impact in your life and the lives of others. Even though I've always been Catholic, I didn't know for years that my faith could be so important! Or maybe you're already really involved with your faith and active in your parish, whether as a volunteer or a full-time worker. You go to Mass every Sunday, and your faith is a big part of your life. Wherever you are, I'm excited to share with you what it means to partake of the Church's mission.

I was raised Catholic by two amazing parents, but my faith didn't really play a big part in my life until I was an adult.

(I'll share more of that story later on.) As I began a personal relationship with Jesus, all I wanted to do was to share Him with other people. I read a lot of books, even studied theology at school. But if there's one thing I've learned since that first moment when I really encountered Jesus and gave my life to Him, it's that sharing your faith doesn't have to be complicated. This isn't just for priests or nuns or people who work for the Church. If you're baptized, this is for you! God has a plan for you and is inviting you to join with Him to advance the mission of the Church. So, I'd like to share with you how I've come to understand what it means to live as a disciple of Jesus in the world, and how to share Him with other people.

My wife, Rosemary, and I once had dinner with a few friends who are making an extraordinary impact in the Church through their work. They've devoted their lives to teaching people about evangelization and discipleship.

Our discussion about our faith journeys turned to my childhood and early memories of the Catholic Church. I shared about my faith experience as a kid and how I was forced to attend Mass. I was on a roll telling this story, and I said, "I hated going to Mass. I mean I didn't just not like it — I hated it!"

Immediately one of my friends interrupted me, "Cande, HATED? That's a strong word. Why did you HATE going to Mass?"

This question stopped me in my tracks. I realized I didn't have a good answer. Still, I did the best I could to explain, and moved on with telling my story. After a good evening, we went our separate ways. Since then, I haven't been able to get that question out of my head. It really stopped me in my tracks. Why was I so insistent on using the word "hate"? Why did I describe my early experiences of being a Catholic with the word *hate*? I didn't *hate* Jesus, but I *hated* going to Mass. Why? I made a list of reasons that I could remember:

- I hated getting up early on a Sunday when I could sleep in.
- I hated having to be quiet and still.
- I hated that I didn't understand any of the readings.
- I hated that I was expected to sing in public and that I felt guilty if I didn't.
- I hated that most of the time when the priest spoke, he was boring and only speaking to adults.
- I hated that I had to kneel and stand. I just wanted to go to sleep.
- I hated that no one spoke to each other and people were territorial about where they sat.
- I hated the music.
- I hated that I felt like I didn't belong, and no one paid attention to me.

As I reflected on this, I thought that surely there must have been some things that I did tolerate — and even enjoy — about Mass when I was a kid. I came up with a list of things that I had enjoyed at Mass in my childhood:

- I enjoyed putting the envelope my dad gave me in the offertory basket.
- I enjoyed holding hands and praying the Our Father.
- I enjoyed shaking hands and saying, "Peace be with you."
- I enjoyed going into the communion line to receive Jesus.
- I enjoyed going to a restaurant to have breakfast after Mass.

At the heart of it, as a child, I really didn't know Jesus. I saw His pictures; I knew He died on the cross and rose from the dead; and I knew that I could talk to Him. But I couldn't understand why Mass was so complicated, and I assumed that the only way to have a relationship with Jesus was by attending and loving Mass. My parents told me, "All Jesus wants is an hour a week." I couldn't even give Him that. In fact, I hated it!

By the time I was a junior in high school, I had stopped attending Mass, and just went if my parents asked me to accompany them. I still acknowledged God at this time in my life, but it was more out of fear of what would happen if I were to die.

Over the next several years, I was able to lessen this fear by just "staying away" from anything having to do with God or church. The less I thought about it, the less real it was. I didn't understand the connection of Jesus as God or Jesus as the Eucharist. I never really sought out an understanding; rather, I just assumed I was a bad Catholic because I had hated Mass as a kid. As far as I was concerned, God was "up there" and I was "down here," and if I didn't do anything too terrible, He wouldn't punish me.

This attitude carried into my marriage, as I saw no value in attending Mass or building a relationship with God. Instead, for many years I focused my energies on trying to survive as a young family. That was enough for me to deal with!

OUR CHURCH TODAY
People share many alarming statistics about the state of the Catholic Church today. Here are just a few examples:

- 69 percent of Catholics believe that the bread and wine in the Eucharist are just that — bread and wine, just symbols of Jesus, and not His true presence.

- 52 percent of all adults who were raised Catholic have left the Church at some point in their lives. Only 4 in 10 have returned.
- Only 64 percent of those who identify as Catholic believe in God.
- 48 percent of Catholics believe abortion should be legal.

Anyone who has worked in any kind of ministry hears these statistics every day. We see it in the pews, in our communities, and in our families. People don't know Jesus, and they don't know His Church. The problem is that people should be coming to know Jesus *through* His Church — yet as these statistics show, far too many Catholics do not seem to know Jesus or to accept His teachings.

Jesus knew all of this would happen; this is part of the reason why He has given each baptized Catholic a mission: "Go therefore and make disciples of all nations, baptizing them in the name of the Father and of the Son and of the Holy Spirit, teaching them to observe all that I have commanded you" (Mt 28:19–20). Our mission is to live this calling every day of our lives. Today we see people seeking to advance the mission of the Church through evangelization and discipleship. We try to create systems that can be easily replicated from parish to parish. We build committees, hire people, and buy programs to help us. To a certain extent, this is necessary. However, we can never lose sight of what this is all about: to help bring people to Jesus.

We usually think that evangelization and discipleship only happen outside the Church walls. While it's true — evangelization has to reach beyond the walls of the Church — we also have a lot of work to do with the people who fill our pews and are registered at our parishes. With this book, I want to share with you three transformational principles that are essential to bringing people to Jesus and advancing His mission for the Church.

These principles were developed after I spent a few days of reflection with my leadership team in the Office of Mission Advancement at the Diocese of Phoenix. During that time, we discerned and reflected together about how God wanted to use our office and what our role was in the mission of the Church. Our office's three key words had always been *stewardship, discipleship*, and *evangelization*. Yet we had found that in the world of Church ministry, those words can mean a lot of things to a lot of different people. So, we spent some time praying and asking God to show us how those words applied to our work, and how He wanted to use us to advance the mission of the Church.

We walked away from that time of prayer with these three transformational principles — principles that are true not just for me and my team, but for anyone who works and ministers in the Church, and for any Christian who wants to live out their baptismal call to share the Gospel. These three principles are:

1. Strengthening relationships
2. Boldly growing engagement
3. Connecting people to the mission

These principles are not necessarily new or earth-shattering. In fact, these were things I'd known throughout my time in ministry and tried to practice, and I think many people in ministry could say the same. But once we articulated these three principles, we had a new, clear understanding of how they tied into our mission.

- Strengthening relationships is really all about being a good **steward** of one of the most important treasures of the Church: people and our relationships with them.

- **Discipleship** is simply inviting people to take the next step in their faith journey and leading them to a deeper relationship with Jesus through His Church — boldly growing engagement.
- Connecting people to the mission is all about inviting others to join the mission of the Church and to encounter the living Christ — that's **evangelization**!

If you work in a diocese or parish, or in any kind of ministry, perhaps your key words to describe your mission are different from ours. That's okay. These transformational principles still apply, because the common factor is people.

People are at the heart of the mission of the Church. Sometimes we are so focused on the process of making disciples, evangelizing, or teaching stewardship that we forget who we are trying to help. We forget every person we serve has a unique place in the mission and a personal story.

Strengthening relationships, boldly growing engagement, and connecting people to the mission are simple ways to bring people to Jesus. It's not complicated — we just need to bring people to Jesus. God is always drawing closer to us, so we can rest assured that He is the one doing the hard work — not us!

In order to bring people to Jesus, we must start with loving and caring for people one at a time. It can't be a numbers game, and it can't be an obligation. It has to come from a genuine desire to love and to show people that they matter. After all, why would anyone listen to the Good News from us, if we haven't shown them God's love? Think of someone in your life who hasn't treated you well. Can you imagine your reaction if they tried to share the Gospel with you? What would you think?

Remember all the things I said that I loved about Mass as a kid? All of these things were relational, engaging, and made me feel a part of something bigger than myself. As a kid I didn't understand what was going on, but now in retrospect I see I was craving to be acknowledged as a person. I wanted to feel like my life had meaning and that I could contribute something.

I believe this is what all people truly desire: to be in authentic relationships with people who genuinely care about them. People want to be engaged with their life in a courageous way that can offer them meaning and purpose. And every one of us at our core wants to be connected to a mission, because we were created to be in communion with people.

HOW TO READ THIS BOOK

You picked up this book, so I suspect you have a desire to help the Catholic Church grow and to give your best to the Lord. I would encourage you to pray and reflect as you read this book. Don't rush through it; spend time considering each chapter and the challenges at the end.

Maybe consider reading this book with your spouse, your colleagues, or fellow ministry members. Read a chapter a week and discuss the challenges together. Help each other through the book. Maybe start a group text so that you can send each other thoughts about your reading throughout the week, and offer one another encouragement as you seek to grow together.

Ultimately, this book is about introducing you to the three transformational principles for mission, which I laid out above, and helping you apply them to your life and work in ministry. These principles seem quite simple, but we know from our own day-to-day experience as Christians that they can be quite challenging. Yet if we truly want things to be different, we must have the attitude of Christ (Phil 2:5). This means, like Jesus, we need to humble ourselves so that we can walk with people and courageously invite them into a relationship with God — not so much through the things we say, but in the way we live our lives, giving all the glory to God.

Part I
CALLED TO MISSION

"For I know the plans I have for you, says the Lord,
plans for welfare and not for evil, to give you a future
and a hope. Then you will call upon me and come
and pray to me, and I will hear you. You will seek
me and find me; when you seek me with all your
heart, I will be found by you, says the Lord, *and I*
will restore your fortunes and gather you from all
the nations and all the places where I have driven
you, says the Lord, *and I will bring you back to*
the place from which I sent you into exile."

Jeremiah 29:11–14

Your life has meaning. Your life has purpose. Your life matters, and you are important. You may not realize it, but people are waiting for you to fulfill your God-given purpose in life. This is your part in the mission of the Church.

In order to step into the Church's mission in an impactful way, however, we first need to discern our place within the Church. There are three fundamental action steps that we need to take in order to live with clarity and joy, and with the confidence and courage to do what God asks of us, even when it seems impossible. These three things are:

- Understanding your identity
- Discovering your purpose
- Learning your role in the mission

Have you ever asked yourself, "What's the meaning of life?" or maybe, "What does God want from me?" These are normal questions, and they don't have easy answers. They take prayer and deep reflection on your own life so that God can reveal what He wants from you. Oftentimes, we are just trying to survive in life — paying the bills, raising the kids, taking care of our health, or working full-time (and more than full-time). So, when we get a free moment, we are too exhausted to really think about these deep questions.

I understand — I have just been trying to survive in this fast-paced world since I was twenty years old. I finally discovered these three steps (knowing my identity, discovering my purpose, and knowing my role in the mission), and they have brought everything together for me. While I wish I had understood this when I was twenty years old, I don't think I was ready then, because I wasn't willing to listen to the Teacher — Jesus.

This book is about helping you live out the three transformational principles described in the introduction (strengthening relationships, boldly growing engagement, and connecting people to the mission). Perhaps it's possible for you to live out these principles without fully understanding your own identity, purpose, and mission, but your growth in these three areas will only be strengthened as you discover more fully what God has in mind for you in your unique, unrepeatable life. What's more, we risk completely missing out on the meaning of our lives if we don't take time to really understand who we are, why we were made, and how God has equipped us to live and serve in a way that no one else can.

So before we explore the transformational principles in depth, I want to pause and reflect on each of these three key steps that will allow us to enter into the heart of the Church's mission with clear vision and great joy.

1

UNDERSTANDING YOUR IDENTITY

Growing up, I was known as a good talker. I could talk my way into (or out of) just about any situation. I'd learned really well from our society to look out for #1 — myself. I was great at figuring out how other people could help me get what I wanted, and I was always thinking, "What's my next move?"

THE "AHA" MOMENT

One day, my best friend in high school introduced me as someone who was the best "b***s****er he'd ever seen" (he used the real word). At first, I felt like this was a compliment. I knew he was right — I was good with words and had a gift for telling people what they wanted to hear.

The more I thought about it, however, the more I wondered

if that was really what I wanted to be known for. I hadn't realized it until that moment, but my ability to BS and manipulate situations to my own advantage had become my identity. This is how people knew me, and I based my self-worth on it. After real reflection on this, I realized I didn't like that. When I left home for the Marine Corps immediately after high school, I made the decision to change that reputation and committed to never lie or mislead again.

I realized that I had just been using people to get what I wanted. I didn't understand how people and relationships could be a gift in my life, not because of what they could do for me, but just because of who they were. By treating interactions as transactions, I was missing out on something better than I ever could have imagined.

Although I didn't realize that God was working in my life, when I look back on that decision, I can see it now as a point of conversion. I saw something in myself that wasn't right and made a decision to change. I call that moment my "aha moment" — when I realized that life might not be all about me. I might not be the center of the universe. Maybe there was something more.

LIFE BEFORE CHRIST

Growing up, I always felt that I was called to something great. I had all these hopes and dreams as a teenager to be successful and to flourish. When I was younger, my dream was to become a United States senator. I thought that in order to get there, I had to focus on myself, to advance myself. As I got older, life began to show me that I spent way too much time focused on me and not enough on the people around me.

That was about to change in an unexpected way. At twenty years old, I was recently married to my wife, Rosemary, and we were pregnant with our first daughter. Two years later, I was out of the Marine Corps, and I really went into survival mode.

I struggled financially while working days in my dad's tire business and going to college at night. Suddenly I had the real responsibility of providing for people other than myself, and I had to make life work. It was a constant financial struggle. It was not uncommon for me to come home to find the power or the water cut off, or to have to plan carefully in order to make sure we could get groceries.

My life felt like it was on autopilot in a constant loop to nowhere. I was working hard, but I still felt very stuck — like there was no light at the end of the tunnel. No matter what I did, we couldn't get ahead of the bills. Throughout all this, I'd done my best to stay true to the decision I'd made when I graduated high school: I would not manipulate people or situations for my own advantage.

One day, about six years after I started working for my dad, I was working as usual at the tire shop. On this particular day, the store was swamped. We were full of customers, and the phones were ringing off the hook. I was overwhelmed to say the least, and in the midst of all this, a regular customer came into the store holding a flat tire. He was a good guy, but he always liked to get the best possible deals for the work we did.

He asked for help repairing the flat, and even though we were so busy, I agreed. I figured it was easier to help him now and get him out of the shop than to do anything else. As I was doing the work, he said, "Cande, I just want you to know that I really appreciate your help, and your family has always been good to me." I mumbled something in response, eager to finish as soon as possible. "It's because of this that I want to give you something," he said. "You've always been good to me, and I am really grateful."

As he spoke, he pulled a car key out of his pocket. This wasn't one of those jangly keys, but the kind where you push a button to get the key to open. I knew it belonged to a nice car. I walked out to the parking lot with him, and he handed me the key to the car — a Mercedes sitting on the back of a trailer.

I couldn't believe he was actually giving it to me. I remember wondering, "What's the catch? Does this car even work?" Then as quickly as I had these thoughts, I felt guilty. I hadn't wanted to serve this man, and I didn't even know his name even though he was a frequent visitor to the shop. Despite my not truly caring about this man, he had just given me a Mercedes! I thanked him. This gift came at a time when my family really needed some extra help.

When I told Rosemary about it, I informed her that I was planning to flip the car, sell it, and pay off some bills. She told me before I did that, I should ask God what he wanted me to do with the car. I looked at her, puzzled, and said, "Sure, no problem." Really, I had no intention of doing that.

Later that week, I was dropping a customer off at a bar. On the street corner, a man stood with a bucket of cleaning supplies looking for work. He shouted out to me and asked if I needed a car wash.

"Do you detail cars?" I asked. "If so, I have a car back at my shop that needs to be cleaned." He agreed to do the work and got in my car to drive back to the shop. As we drove, he told me that his name was Nate and he was trying to make some extra money to pay his electric bill, or else it would get shut off on him. He had a wife and kids and had just lost his job. Even though he told me that, I still managed to negotiate a lower rate for his work. (Sadly, this was still a big part of who I was!) I asked him what kind of work he usually did. He said that he was a mechanic, and if he ever managed to save enough money for a car, he wanted to start a mechanic-on-wheels business.

I got Nate set up cleaning the Mercedes I'd just received. As I walked back to my office to wait for him to finish, I remembered what Rosemary told me the night before. I still had to ask God what He wanted me to do with the car. So, to be faithful to my word, under my breath I half-heartedly prayed, "God, what do You want me to do with this car?"

Then this thought immediately popped into my head: "You know what you're supposed to do with it." Those words definitely weren't from me. But it was true. I knew in my heart that I was supposed to give Nate the car. I struggled with this. Why would God want me to give my new car to a man I just met on a street corner? I was already doing good by giving him work!

When Nate finished cleaning the car, he came inside the shop to collect his payment for the work. I asked him to sit down, and I paid him his wage. Then I told him I had spoken to God, and God wanted to help him. What I said next went something like this: "Nate, this sounds crazy, but God told me He wants to help you. So I'm going to give you this car with the title and consider it your tip. But I want you to know — I'm not giving it to you. God is." Nate just broke down crying in disbelief. I cried with him, and we hugged each other before he left.

After he was gone, I just sat there in my office wondering what in the world I'd just done, and how I could have done something as crazy as giving away a car just because I listened to a voice inside of me. I questioned if I really heard God, or if it was just me.

It's important to explain that at this time in my life, I had no personal relationship with God. But I knew this was God working through me, because I would never have given away the car on my own. Somehow, I just knew that the car didn't belong to me. I was Catholic and went to church on Sunday, because Rosemary wanted me to. But I certainly didn't know God or ever think too much about His plan for my life. Never did I think that God would actually speak to me.

From that day when I first heard God's voice and gave Nate the car, blessings began in our lives. Cars were coming in, and

I was selling them. Rosemary and I started our own consulting business. Then came the day I'll never forget.

MOMENT OF CONVERSION

December 1, 2006. It was the night that changed my life forever. It was a first Friday, and it was the day Rosemary and I launched our own business. I woke up at two o'clock in the morning and felt compelled to read a book my dad had given me, called *The Richest Man Who Ever Lived*, about King Solomon. I searched for it but couldn't find it. Then I remembered the Book of Proverbs in the Bible was said to have been written by King Solomon. So I found the Bible that Rosemary had given me for our first Valentine's Day. I had never opened it until that night. I remembered she'd told me that before I read the Bible, I should pray for wisdom from the Holy Spirit. I had nothing to lose, so I did just that and started reading Proverbs.

Within the first few verses in the beginning of Proverbs, I was stopped in my tracks: "The fear of the LORD is the beginning of knowledge; fools despise wisdom and instruction" (Prov 1:7). I was paralyzed and just read that verse over and over. I realized in that moment that I was a fool, because I did not fear the Lord. I wasn't afraid of not having Him in my life, because I didn't fear Him, and this is why I had no wisdom.

As I read, I encountered God in Scripture in a way that I never had before. He became alive to me. That night, I decided to stop being a fool and to seek God above everything else. I wanted to know what His will was for my life. Just like I'd asked Him what to do with that car, now I was asking Him what to do with my life. I had this burning desire in my heart to evangelize, even though I didn't really know what that meant. Rosemary encouraged me to keep praying, to keep asking what God wanted me to do, and to do whatever that was.

For me, doing whatever God wanted made me look a little

crazy. Because I had spent so long trying to be the one in charge, I think that God had to take some drastic steps to teach me to trust Him with my whole heart. Early on in my walk with Him, I felt like He wanted me to focus all my energy on getting to know Him and on seeking His will for my life. So, as a father with a wife and three kids, I quit focusing on my own business and spent the next several months focusing on God. I am so grateful for Rosemary's support during that time. Even as we maxed out our credit cards and food was starting to run short, she always supported me and believed right along with me that God was going to lead me and take care of our family.

We spent about six months praying and seeking God's guidance. I would just ask Him to use me. I told God I didn't want my own business anymore. I wanted to work for Him. I would do anything, even mow His lawn (the one at the church) if He told me to. Finally, one Monday, Rosemary reached a breaking point and told me that I had to do something soon, or else there wouldn't be any food for our family. I was still waiting on God's direction, and so I got down on my knees in my daughter's bedroom and begged God for help. I asked Him what to do and how to provide for my family. Then I said, "I want to rely on You. I need Your help!" Just like the time I'd given the car to Nate, I heard his voice again clearly: "*Wait until Wednesday.*"

I told Rosemary, "I had a conversation with God. Give me two days. He'll provide for us."

The next day, I got a call from a local school. They'd heard I had a consulting company and asked if I would be willing to work with them. By the next day (Wednesday), I had a contract to work with them. It took two days — just like God had said! I'm still amazed at how God provides for me. That experience taught me in a real way that, even though I was an adult, I had to live like a child, totally reliant on God for everything. I learned that trusting in the Lord isn't just a nice idea, but a real choice and an action.

A COMMON THREAD

I share these two stories with you because it was these two ex-periences that were the beginning of my personal conversion. Prior to these experiences, my identity was tied up in how much money I made and how successful I was. God had to challenge me to trust in Him more than myself. I had to learn to trust in Him as my Father. Once I realized that I was a child of God, my whole life changed. I realized that He had a plan for my life — He loved me and would always provide for me.

What I've learned since then is that, if I'm a child of God, that means everyone else is too. We're all in this together, and I believe that God gives us to each other to help us on our journey, just like my brief interaction with Nate, which helped me listen to God in a way I never had before. In all those years before, when I thought everything was all about me, I didn't realize what I was missing. This is just the danger that a lot of us fall into. My life was going okay. I had an amazing wife, beautiful daughters, a good job, and even though we sometimes struggled to make ends meet, we were paying the bills. I had no idea that recogniz-ing my identity as a son of God and member of His family could have such a profound impact on my life.

When our identity is found in God, we begin to see our re-lationships differently. There is a common thread that draws us all together: Jesus. He does that in some pretty fantastic ways.

If we're all God's children, then we have a responsibility to help each other. We're meant to live in relationship, and to be the living presence of God in the world — to show His love to the people around us. This means treating people like family, not transactions. It's easy to do this with the people we enjoy being around. It's a lot harder to put into practice when we're talking about a coworker or acquaintance who drives us crazy. But like it or not, we're all called to this.

For me, this was a revolutionary idea: I'm not better than

anyone else. The world tries to separate us all the time by putting us into categories of race, gender, or socioeconomic status. Those don't really matter. We're all children of God. That is our identity, not anything else we have or do.

CHALLENGE

This concept may be as transformational for you as it was for me. It's important for all of us to try to see the people in front of us and love them like Jesus does. I invite you to join me in that, to strive each day to see people as your brothers and sisters and to treat them accordingly.

I encourage you to spend some time in prayer, reflecting on these questions:

- What am I holding on to? Where do I need to surrender control to God and let Him take care of me?
- Where do I find my identity? Is it in something I do? Something I have? Why?
- Who are the people right in front of me who are hardest to love?

These are hard questions to ask ourselves, and even harder to answer. As you pray, I also suggest you ask God for the particular grace you need — to surrender, to love, to find your identity in Him.

2

DISCOVERING YOUR PURPOSE

Having a conversion and understanding that we are children of God is only the first step in understanding why we were created. The Church says we were created to know, love, and serve God. That's true. We were. But how do we do that? God didn't make us to be robots, but He created each of us with a specific mission, a purpose to live out in this life. To help us fulfill that mission, He's given each of us the gifts and talents we need in order to be successful. The gifts He has given you are unique — unlike anyone else's. They're kind of like a spiritual thumbprint.

Stop and think about that for a minute: You have talents and skills that are unlike anyone else's. I used to think that I didn't have any special talents. I was looking for things that were obvious, like a great singing voice, athletic prowess, unusual intelligence, or a great sense of comedy. Yet I wasn't really skilled in any of these areas.

Still, when I was growing up, teachers used to tell me, "You're so talented!" I didn't see where they got that. I can be really hard on myself sometimes, so all I could see were the things I wasn't good at.

In seventh grade, I had a teacher named Mrs. Burke. One day she said to me, "You're really good at presenting. You should try doing this more often." I wasn't that interested until she told me that I could enter a contest to win $250. I decided to give it a shot, and with very little preparation, I ended up winning! It wasn't even that hard for me. I started to understand that I had a gift for public speaking. I don't get nervous in front of crowds, and I can do pretty well at speaking without much preparation. It's also something I enjoy.

I think all of us have gifts like this. There are certain things that no one else can do like you can. It took me a long time to recognize this. Public speaking is one of the gifts that God has given me, but it's not just for myself. It's to help fulfill the purpose for which He created me, to have an impact on others, to help me grow as a person, and to be His witness in the world. Wherever you are in life, as long as you're using your gifts and talents to serve God, you can make a difference!

So how do we discover our gifts?

DISCOVERING YOUR GIFTS

Rosemary makes the best chicken tacos I've ever had in my life. They're unlike anyone else's. People come over to our house, just hoping that she'll make her chicken tacos. The recipe is so simple: chicken, lettuce, tomato, cheese, and avocado on a corn tortilla. But when Rosemary makes them, there's something special about them that keeps people coming back for more. The key is,

I think, that Rosemary's the one making them, and her love goes into making them. She has a gift for that, unlike anyone else's.

Although it may seem silly, I think this is a good example of how we can all learn to identify our gifts. When God gives us a gift, it just comes naturally to us. Like Rosemary's tacos and my public speaking, we didn't have to try very hard to make them turn out well. They just did. Take a minute and think about that. What is it that you do that just turns out really well — better than when others around you try to do the same thing in the same way? Make a list!

Now read back through your list. What do you see there that you love to do? This is often another way that we can discover our gifts. God doesn't give us skills that will make us miserable in life. The gifts He gives us help us to fulfill our purpose and also bring us joy and fulfillment. What do you love doing? What would you do every day, even if you weren't getting paid? Is it music? Teaching? Taking care of sick people? Fixing cars? If you look closely, I bet you'll see that what you love doing and what you're gifted at are pretty similar.

DISCOVERING YOUR PURPOSE

Your God-given purpose in life is most likely a combination of those two things: your gifts and your passions. As much as I loved working for my dad in his tire store, it wasn't fulfilling my purpose. That's why Rosemary started challenging me to do what I love. She told me I needed to practice my gifts, otherwise I might lose them. I knew I was good at public speaking and I loved helping people. After a year of planning and preparation, Rosemary and I made a business plan, saved up an emergency fund, and made sure our family would be okay during the time of transition. We started a business called Your Journey Now. My mission was to help people discover their purpose in life. In the end, it didn't work out as well as I'd expected. I don't call it a failure, though, because it was the first step I needed to take in order to get to where I am now. Along the way, I did see that using my gifts was making an impact in the world.

One night, while we were still running Your Journey Now, I was holding a seminar at a local hotel. I'd reserved a meeting room that could hold several hundred people. By the night of the event, only a couple dozen people had registered. I was at the hotel preparing myself to talk to a small crowd in a big room when I ran into another guest. He was staying there on vacation with his adult daughter. Eager to fill more seats, I invited them to join us for the evening. Surprisingly, he agreed, and both were there that night. At the end of my presentation, I opened the floor for comments or questions. The man's daughter stood up and started sharing a story about how her father hadn't been around when she was growing up. She shared a traumatic experience that happened to her during her childhood, without her father in her life. Then she spoke about how glad she was to be able to reconnect with her biological father as an adult. Watching the two of them hugging and crying in the aisle was not how I expected that seminar to end. When I started my business, I expected to help people on the surface level. I never realized that by using my gifts and talents, I could help a father and daughter experience this kind of breakthrough in their relationship during my seminar.

I realized then that my gifts could have an impact. If I had not put my talents to use, this may not have happened. You can have this same kind of impact in the world. I tell my girls all the time: People are waiting for you. There are people in the world who need you to use your gifts and talents. Even if you don't think you have anything to offer, God has given you specific gifts that people need you to use!

If you struggle to identify what your gifts and talents are, perhaps consider some of the following questions:

- What do you love to do? What comes easily to you? What do you have fun doing?
- Has anyone ever told you that you're good at something? What was it?
- If you have extra time, what do you spend it thinking about or doing?
- What do you get excited about? What do you enjoy learning about?

These questions should also inspire us to think of those around us. How can we encourage others in our lives by pointing out what their gifts and talents are? Sometimes people have been discouraged by the world (sometimes by their own family or friends) and may be questioning what their own gifts and talents are.

Reflecting on these questions can reveal some answers for us. Once we have learned what our skills, talents, passions, and gifts are, we can then ask God to show us the pattern and what purpose He wants us to use them for.

It's important to note, though, that just because we enjoy doing something doesn't necessarily mean that it's our calling in life. I love to sing, even though I may not get the rhythm, the tune, or even the words right. It's something I enjoy, if I'm honest, I can also admit that I don't really have the talent to do it well. Pursuing a career as a musician wouldn't be a smart move for me. With that said, we should embrace the things we enjoy, but be clear that they should not distract us from what our true calling in life is.

There are many different ways that God can use our talents to help others. I want to emphasize this: God gave us talents, not for us to use selfishly, but to serve others. The people in our lives are there for a purpose, and we're meant to help them. At the end of the day, our life's purpose is to help other people. The inverse of this is also true: We should also be able to receive help from others who feel called to serve us. When we allow others to help us, we are giving them a chance to use their God-given gifts and realize their life's purpose.

I think about my baseball coaches growing up. They were good at the sport and understood it really well, but they didn't have the skill to play professionally. I don't think they were meant to do that. They were meant to do what they did: to put the skill they had to good use in helping young kids like myself learn to play and to master the discipline of sports.

It requires time in prayer and reflection to discern how God might be calling us to use our gifts. We might not get it right the first time, and we may have to work through some false starts like I did with my business. While it wasn't as successful as I had planned, I know God was using me, nonetheless. Taking the risk of quitting my secure job was a first step toward using my gifts and talents. It started a journey for me and my family that ultimately led me to where I am now.

For many of us, it's not too difficult to figure out what we love to do and what we're good at. Taking the first step toward doing something about it is the challenge.

THE FIRST STEP

Stepping out of your comfort zone is risky. I was comfortable in my job with my dad, but in order to live my purpose, I had to step away from that and start putting to good use the gifts and talents I had. I'd taken the time to learn what I loved and what I was good at, and I made a plan to use those gifts. Finally, I had to execute the plan.

That last step can be terrifying. It might mean leaving your job, moving across the country, going back to school, or losing a regular paycheck. That's why I encourage you to exercise both prudence and courage when making life changes like this. Once

I realized I needed to take a step, I didn't quit my job right away. Rosemary and I took a year to solidify a business plan and build some savings to fall back on if our business didn't immediately turn a profit. Once we had that set up, we took our step. Still, it was scary, and there were times when I doubted that I was doing the right thing. You'll probably experience that too.

It's also important to note that taking a step to discover your purpose might not always mean a career change. You might be already living your purpose in your professional life. Even if you are, I challenge you to think and pray about ways God can use you to help others. I believe that God gives us talents and puts desires in our hearts for a reason: to lead us to our purpose. I never had a desire to be an astronaut or a fireman, so I knew that wasn't my purpose. If you have a love for teaching, maybe that means volunteering in an after-school program or mentoring a younger professional. Maybe your love of music could lead you to join a choir. There are many ways God wants to use us.

However you determine your gifts and talents, whatever you discern God is calling you to do, I want to encourage you again: Do not be afraid to act! Once you take the first step in trust, God will start to open more doors for you. In the parable of the talents (cf. Mt 25:14–30), it's only the servants who invest what they're given who see a return. It's the same for us. When we use what we're given for God's glory, we will see it return with increase. As we're faithful, God will open more doors and give us greater opportunities to serve others. We just have to take the first step.

One piece of advice: That dream or idea that has consumed your thoughts for most of your life is no coincidence. You didn't come up with that on your own. God has placed that in your heart. It can't move from your heart unless you ask God to help you and show you the way. You have to protect this dream, because it doesn't belong to anyone else but you — God gave it to you! That doesn't mean it will be easy, but if you take that first step in trust and ask God to help you persevere, He will help you. Seeking to do God's will is a journey, and it starts with recognizing the desires that He has placed in your heart to bring you where you are meant to be.

CHALLENGE

I challenge you to spend time prayerfully discerning how God is calling you. Pray with holy boldness, trusting that God *is* calling you and has given you amazing gifts to serve others. It might take a period of time to discern His calling. Be patient, persevere in prayer, and trust in Him and His timing.

I invite you to pray and reflect on the following questions:

- What do I believe my purpose in life might be, based on the gifts and talents God has given me?
- Am I doing what I love every day, whether as part of my career or on the side?
- If doing what I love is part of my day job, would I even do it for free? Why or why not?
- What do I think my "next step" might be? Is it drastic (like a career change) or a small step I need to take in my daily life and relationships?
- What am I afraid of when it comes to taking the next step?
- Aside from fear, what else is preventing me from taking the next step?

3

YOUR ROLE IN THE MISSION

Now that you've identified what your gifts and talents are, it's up to God to show you why He gave them to you. The more you discover about your purpose, the more fully you will be able to realize your role in the mission of the Church. In order to do that, we also need to understand what that mission is. In Matthew 28:19–20, right before Jesus ascends into heaven, He clearly tells His disciples what the mission of the Church is: "Go therefore and make disciples of all nations, baptizing them in the name of the Father and of the Son and of the Holy Spirit, teaching them to observe all that I have commanded you." These last two verses of Matthew's Gospel are often referred to as the Great Commission. Let's take some time to break this open.

EVANGELIZING

The first thing Jesus says in the Great Commission is to go and make disciples. What does this mean? It means to invite people into a relationship with Jesus. Next, Jesus tells His followers to baptize those to whom they preach. This means He wants them to become members of His Church and to live out the Christian mission themselves.

The Great Commission was not just for the apostles; it is for all of us Christians, until the end of time. In order to grow the Church, we need to make disciples. Jesus built the Church on the solid rock of Saint Peter (cf. Mt 16:18), and He sent out His disciples to bring people into the Church. It's our job to reach out to others and invite them into the Church Jesus established. The Church isn't just for the people who are already a part of it. We need to be constantly going out to others and sharing Jesus with them. That's what it means to be on mission: We're always looking for a way to share the Good News of what Jesus has done for us.

Sometimes people think that going on mission means going to another country and preaching there or helping those in need. As Catholics, we can fall into the trap of thinking that preaching the Gospel is for priests, deacons, and religious sisters and brothers, and that there's not much for the rest of us to do. Yet the reality is that all of us are called to preach the Gospel — to evangelize. This is what it means to be on mission. We may not do this through preaching with our words; in fact, most of us are called to be on mission in a very simple way. We're called to minister to the people who are already in our lives. We are called to reveal Jesus to them simply in the way we live our lives.

My former pastor, Monsignor Morgan Rowsome, always reminded us that we should be a living witness of Jesus. He would say, "Who you are at home with your family is who you really are." Ask yourself: Can my family and friends tell that I'm a follower of Jesus Christ by the way I live my life? They might hear the words of the Gospel coming out of my mouth, but can they actually see that witness in how I live?

Before we can live the mission, we need to start with ourselves — with our personal holiness. I don't remember my baptism, but sometimes I wish I did. It must have been an awesome moment when Jesus washed my soul and set me free from sin. I'm grateful to my parents for making that choice for me and for raising me in the Faith.

Even though I was baptized as an infant, I talk a lot about my "conversion." This was the time as an adult when I made the decision for myself to be a follower of Jesus and to live my life for Him. Maybe some of you never had that moment. Perhaps you feel that you have always followed Jesus, because you've been faithful to the Church's teachings and have never strayed. That's a beautiful gift! But I invite you to stop and reflect on your life: Do you follow God with your whole heart? Do you consider Jesus truly your friend?

Or perhaps you simply have not yet made the conscious decision to give your whole life to God. There's no time like now! It starts with a simple yes, and then I can assure you, God will do the rest over time.

No matter where you are in your life of faith, I'd like to invite you to pray this prayer from your heart before we go on:

Dear heavenly Father, I am truly sorry for all the sins I have committed. I ask, dear God, that You please forgive me and help lead me to do Your will. I believe in Your son, Jesus Christ. I believe that He suffered, died, and was buried and rose again for the forgiveness of my sins. I ask that He help me to live a life that will give you all the honor and glory. I trust in You, Father, Son, and Holy Spirit. Amen.

If we want to be part of the mission of the Church, we need to consciously choose to live our lives every day for Christ.

DISCIPLESHIP

How you live your life is key to the second part of the Great Commission, where Jesus tells us how to make disciples: "[Teach] them to observe all that I have commanded you." Discipling others is all about teaching them how to live the life that Jesus calls us to live — and this is something we most likely learned from other people who were examples of faith to us. In order to teach people, we first have to know how to do it ourselves. I hear a lot of people say they're afraid to talk about Jesus because they don't have the answers to some of the hard questions that people ask. That's a real struggle, and one that I relate to. But I always tell people two things in response to that: First, you don't have to have all the right answers. It is okay to say, "I don't know." The second thing is that you should be learning what you do not know. We should always be learning and growing in our faith.

Maybe you don't know where to start. After all, there's a lot to learn! In His ministry on earth, Jesus gave us a new commandment. I'd recommend you start with that one, because it's all about learning how to love people: "A new commandment I give to you, that you love one another; even as I have loved you, that you also love one another" (Jn 13:34). This is one of the most important things to remember about living a life on mission: The focus should not be on ourselves. It should be about others. We have been given a mission for others, to help them and bring them to Jesus. Take some time to reflect on Jesus' command. How did He love us? How does that mean we should love others?

YOUR ROLE IN THE MISSION

After I had my conversion, I was on fire for Jesus. I wanted everyone to know Him, and I was desperate to find a way to share the Good News with as many people as would listen to me. But I had always thought only priests had the opportunity to evangelize, so I had a really hard time figuring out how a married man could evangelize.

I went to visit my wife's uncle, who was a Baptist pastor. I told him how much I wanted to evangelize and that I was willing to leave the Catholic Church to become a Protestant pastor if that's what it took for me to be able to evangelize. He told me that's not how God works. Instead, he said God wanted to use me where I was, and that opportunities and paths would open for me to fulfill the desire of my heart. He told me to go to my priest and tell him everything that I had just told him.

He was right. I went to Monsignor Morgan, the pastor of my parish, who became instrumental in my life. He showed me how God could use me to evangelize, starting with my family.

Looking back on my experience, I want to urge you not to think that your role in the mission is any greater or less than anyone else's. God has given each of us a calling and a purpose, including you. We compare ourselves to other people all the time. I don't think we can help it. It's just a human thing. But if we want to be part of the mission of the Church, we need to avoid comparison. He's given you the gifts and talents He needs you to have to fulfill your role in His mission. Think about that for a minute. That means your life has great significance! You have a God-given mission in this world, which only you can carry out. That also means that other people are counting on you to fulfill that role.

CHALLENGE

I invite you to recommit yourself to the mission that God has given each of us in the Church: to go forth and make disciples. If you haven't already made such a commitment, I invite you to pray about it and ask for the grace to do so now. Pray for God's guidance in using the gifts and talents He has given you, and ask Him to open the doors for you to fulfill your role in His mission. As you pray about your role in the mission of the Church, I invite you to reflect on the following questions:

- How do I see myself in the Church's mission? What is my role? Do I believe that I have one?
- Is my life focused on others? What might I need to change to begin to focus a bit more on others and a bit less on myself?
- Who am I with my family? Can even those closest to me see Jesus in me?

Part II
STRENGTHENING RELATIONSHIPS

"You did not choose me, but I chose you and appointed you that you should go and bear fruit and that your fruit should abide; so that whatever you ask the Father in my name, he may give it to you. This I command you, to love one another."

John 15:16–17

The first of the three transformational principles for advancing the mission of the Church is Strengthening Relationships. Relationships are the greatest gifts that God has given us. We need people in our lives, and the relationships that God has given us are not coincidences.

God gives us everything we need. This includes people! In fact, the specific relationships God has given us remind us that everything we need to move the mission forward is right in front of us. When we get into "mission mode," whether it's in our family, job, ministry, or parish, we can easily fall into the mentality that we need things or money to move the mission forward. But what we really need first and foremost is people. God has placed everyone in our lives for a reason. They are meant to walk with us on our journey to heaven and to help us fulfill the mission that He has given us. All we have to do is ask God to bring forward the relationships in our lives that can help us supply our every need for the mission.

We can look to the model Jesus gave us. The Bible tells us that He spent three years preaching, feeding, healing, walking, laughing, crying, and building relationships with people.

It is especially important to recognize that in His relationship with each of the apostles, He was building friendship, trust, authenticity, and vulnerability, which laid the groundwork for these men to be sent on mission. After He spent time with them, they were able to understand the profoundness of His life, death, and resurrection, and they would go on to change the world.

4

RELATIONSHIPS START WITH FAMILY

A FAMILY OF RELATIONSHIPS

I come from a Mexican-American family that was all about family dinner and conversations at the table. I loved those discussions, filled with laughter, strong opinions, disagreements, and tons of stories. This was the time when my parents would enter into real dialogue with us. Around the dinner table they treated us kids like adults, listening and trying to understand our thoughts.

At one dinner when I was in second grade, my younger sister Kelly (who was also in second grade) shared that she was being picked on at school. She said the kids would make fun of her and she felt all alone. She was scared that she would get beat up. As I was scarfing down my mom's tortillas, my dad asked,

"Did you know about this?" I shook my head no.

He then asked me, "Why don't you know? You are in the same grade and the same class. How in the world did you not know this is happening to your sister?"

I answered, "I don't know. It's none of my business."

My dad got very upset, and Kelly started crying. He told me, "This is completely unacceptable. You are not just your sister's brother, you are her big brother! You are her family. That means the same blood that runs through her runs through you."

I tried to defend myself. "But, Dad," I said, "If I stick up for her, then I might get beat up too!"

This made my dad even angrier. He said, "I don't care if you get beat up! Your job is to always take care of your family and to defend your sister at all costs, even your own well-being!"

This was a valuable lesson for me in what it means to be selfless toward others. Although the other person in this situation was my sister, I understand why this fundamental principle of caring for and defending your family was so important. My dad knew that if I couldn't learn this basic lesson of love for my biological sister, then I could never learn to love others who were not my family. He was teaching me a lesson that's found in Scripture: "We love, because he first loved us. If anyone says, 'I love God,' and hates his brother, he is a liar; for he who does not love his brother whom he has seen, cannot love God whom he has not seen. And this commandment we have from him, that he who loves God should love his brother also" (1 Jn 4:19–21).

I don't think my dad realized that what he taught us as kids was something the apostle John also tried to teach to the early Church. Even so, my dad was right — God expects us to love the people in our lives, just as we love Him!

Because of our baptism, we are all connected. We are all made family. We are truly incorporated into the Body of Christ, and thus we share common blood that runs through all of us and makes us children of God. It becomes our responsibility to care for our brothers and sisters in Christ. It should bother us when we meet someone who is in need or unloved. That's the new commandment Jesus left us with: "love one another; even as I have loved you, that you also love one another" (Jn 13:34).

That's not always easy. There are always people in our lives who can be a challenge to live with. It's hard to see them as brothers or sisters in Christ, and it's hard to want to help them. Yet I've learned over the years that it's the people who frustrate me the most who also help me grow the most.

This is why we have to be especially attentive to difficult relationships. These relationships require us to put forth an effort to choose to love. They also lead us along the path of true holiness and help us in our mission.

I try to remind myself that, since each person is God's creation, loving others is loving God. The same applies even if they're not Christian. I have no way of knowing where a person is on their journey with God. Even if they're not baptized, they're still beloved by God, and He is still at work in their lives, drawing them closer to Him.

IT STARTS WITH FAMILY

The relationships we experienced as children established a foundation for our relationships as adults. It's important to spend time reflecting on how our families taught us about what it means to be in relationship. What lessons have you gained from your family? What values did you learn? What relationship skills did you develop? Speaking as a parent, I can say from experience — as much as parents, guardians, and siblings may try, we don't do everything right.

So, if your family is normal, this means that you also experienced hurt or disappointment from those you loved and trusted most. It's important to recognize the ways in which you were hurt or wounded as a child. This can help you to understand some of the perceptions or expectations you have about relationships now. Recognizing hurt can also help heal relationships as we learn to forgive.

It's important to recognize that even the best human relationships will eventually cause us hurt in some way. I am not trying to sound disappointing, but it's the honest truth. The solution to that isn't to avoid people altogether or to cut them out of our lives, if and when they hurt us. God, knowing that we're not perfect and would make mistakes, made us to be in relationship with each other and with Him. And if God, Who is perfect, can keep pursuing a relationship with each one of us, even when we fail, shouldn't we do the same for others — especially since we ourselves are not perfect?

We have to be willing to be a part of people's lives, and to let them be a part of ours, accepting who they are and recognizing their life as a gift. In order to really let people in, we have to practice trust, humility, vulnerability, and authenticity. This is hard! It's hard to keep on trusting people, especially when we've been hurt before. It's also hard to have the courage to show people who we really are, with all our faults and weaknesses. It's hard to admit that we're not perfect or that we need help. But in order to build real relationships, this is vital!

This is not to say that you should allow people to continuously hurt you or take advantage of you. It is important that we teach people how we expect to be treated and create healthy boundaries.

RELATIONSHIPS TO ADVANCE THE MISSION

Because of our baptism, we already have a relationship with every Catholic (those alive now and those who have gone before us and are now in heaven or in purgatory). Think about that for a minute: Every baptized person is part of the family of God. You are too! This means that we are all related. We are all family. Even so, as I've traveled to different parishes, I have noticed that it can be difficult for pastors, parish staff, and ministry leaders to see the connection between this family relationship we share, and our call to be part of advancing the mission of the Church.

Especially for those who work for a parish and in ministry, it's easy to fall into the pattern of seeing our fellow Catholics as people who fill the pews and help pay to keep the lights on. We begin to act as though people exist only to help the Church. In reality, it is the opposite: The Church exists for the people of God, to be the means that brings them closer to Him. As the family of God, we are here for each other. We are here to help each other along the journey of this life. In order to help us do that, let's reflect on the following questions:

- Do I believe that God has placed the right people in my life to help me fulfill His purpose for my life?
- The Church is a group of people, not a collection of things. Where do I put the most value — on things and money or on people?
- Am I inviting others to help in the mission?

The people who are closest to us might answer these questions about us differently than we would ourselves. This is one of the reasons why relationships are so important to the mission. We need each other, especially when it comes to realizing how we make others feel. I think sometimes we can have a blind spot and not see ourselves clearly, but the people we trust can help us see ourselves as we really are. I think of my family as a perfect example of this. My sisters and I have all done well in our lives, but when we get together, we are quick to call each other out if one of us gets too big of a head!

I think we also need to remember that even Jesus didn't work alone. He's God. He could have single-handedly preached the Gospel and built up the Church in the thirty-three years He spent on earth. But He didn't. During His three years of earthly ministry, He was constantly sending people out to preach, to teach, and to heal. He didn't have to, but He chose to do so because He wanted people to be involved in the mission of the Church. That hasn't changed. God still wants people engaged and participating in the mission of the Church to "go forth and make disciples." By allowing people into our teams and into our work, we are inviting them into the mission of the Church. What an awesome gift to give someone!

When we work for the Church or have spent a long time volunteering for a particular ministry, sometimes it can be difficult to invite people to join us in the mission. We become protective of our responsibilities and reluctant to let anyone help. This is especially true when we have been in a particular role for a while. At times, we prefer to keep control, because we know exactly how we want something done. If we delegate, there's a chance it'll get done differently or imperfectly.

It's important to remember that it's nearly impossible to grow into new and greater responsibilities if we are not willing to let go of the responsibilities we have now. At some point, we are going to have to let someone else help.

Imagine if you got promoted at work and didn't want to stop doing your old job to accept a new role in your organization. You would never advance or grow, and you might stand in the way of good opportunities for others. It's the same in ministry. In order to assume a new role, we need to let others take over. We need to have the humility to realize that our way is not the only way, and just because someone does things differently doesn't mean it's wrong.

You might be saying to yourself, "This sounds hard! Why

should I bother doing all this work to strengthen relationships? It's just easier to work alone." As an answer, I think of my bishop. He's a wonderful, saintly man who's responsible for the 1.2 million Catholics who live in the Diocese of Phoenix. He makes no secret of the fact that he can't bear that responsibility on his own. He relies on the staff of the Diocesan Pastoral Center and the priests, deacons, their wives, the staff, and thousands of volunteers who serve throughout the diocese to help him to do his job. He understands that we are the body of Christ and, as a body, we need to work together in order to get anything done.

I couldn't agree with our bishop more! Our relationships in ministry are essential, because we are all working for the same mission. We cannot do it alone, and we need each other.

A DIFFERENT PERSPECTIVE

When working in mission, we will probably find ourselves working with people who do not share our perspective. When this happens, we must remember that their past influences their perspective today, just as our past experiences impact our perspectives. Each of us is in a different place when it comes to building trust, being vulnerable, being humble, and remaining authentic. Recognizing this makes it easier to see why others might think, act, or speak differently than we do.

This is the first step in understanding and loving others: We need to recognize that their perspective is not necessarily wrong. It's the reality they live in. This is especially important when they may not understand the Church's teachings or the administrative reality of the Church.

At the same time, our own perspective can cause challenges for us. Because it is our reality, it can blind us and keep us from hearing what people are trying to say to us. Sometimes what is offered as constructive feedback can be received as criticism.

Rosemary once told me that when people give her parenting advice, she sometimes hears it as criticism and feels like what they are really telling her is that she is a bad mom. Someone else I know told me something similar — she is so worried about doing a good job in her career that when she receives suggestions or advice, she often feels people are being critical of her. It's important to be honest with ourselves and have the self-awareness to not let our own perspectives affect our relationships.

Thinking back to why I loved our family dinner growing up — it was because my parents didn't treat us like kids. They were building a relationship based on the understanding that we had different experiences and perspectives than they did. So rather than argue or belittle, they listened, encouraged, and taught us with love (even when it had to be tough love, sometimes). When working with others, it is important that we use the simple technique that my parents did: Listen, encourage, and teach with love.

CHALLENGE

Relationships are important because we were made for them, and we can't make it through this life without them. I want to challenge you to think of two people:

- Someone with whom you have a really strong relationship. Spend some time reflecting on what helped make your relationship so strong. What moments of vulnerability or trust have you experienced? How has your relationship grown over the years?
- Someone with whom you struggle to have a relationship. Spend some time reflecting on why there is a struggle there. Have you siloed yourself? Are you letting your perspective block you from being open to theirs? What is the difference between this

relationship and the previous one you were reflecting on? How can you be intentional about building this relationship?

5
MADE FOR RELATIONSHIPS

After I came to know Jesus, I felt like He was inviting me to spend time in Eucharistic adoration. I knew nothing about adoration, so I would sit in front of the Blessed Sacrament and stare. Anybody who knows me knows I can barely sit still. But I took a leap of faith and signed up for the 3:00 p.m. hour each Thursday, when our parish held weekly adoration. I had no idea what was in store for me.

Weekly adoration at my parish was held in a cry room converted into a small chapel. When I showed up for my first hour, no one else was there except one older lady sitting two pews back from the monstrance. She sat completely still, arms crossed.

For months I went to my adoration hour and, week after week, this woman was always there before I got there. I had learned her name was Joyce. She appeared to be much older and must have weighed less than 100 pounds.

Every week, I would stay for exactly one hour — never more and never less. Joyce never spoke or moved, but she was always there before I got there and was still there when I left, gazing at our Lord. I began to look forward to adoration, just to see Joyce and ask God to make me like her. I'm not sure why I prayed that, but it was so apparent that she had a deep love for the Lord. After months, one day when I showed up for adoration, she wasn't there. I knew something must have happened.

I called the parish secretary and asked her if something had happened to Joyce, since she wasn't at adoration. She told me that Joyce had passed away. I was heartbroken. Somehow, I felt connected to Joyce. I decided to go to the rosary service held for her at our parish. Coincidentally, it was on a Thursday — the same day that she and I had shared our adoration time. When I arrived, I noticed all the Thursday adorers were present at the back of the church, along with all the men and women who had attended daily Mass with her. She had only a small group of family members present. In fact, there were more adorers and daily Mass attendees there than anyone else.

The Rosary was led by our pastor, who spoke about how Joyce loved Jesus and her parish family, and about how she was a witness to God's love by the way she lived her life. I was very emotional, mourning the loss of this person to whom I had never spoken a word.

Our pastor concluded the Rosary by saying, "I am going to do something that I've never done before. I'm going to let Joyce rest in the presence of the Lord in the adoration chapel tonight, since this is where she was most at peace." Her casket was placed in the adoration chapel, and she was left in the chapel with Jesus all night.

Joyce's story reminds me of how we are made to be in relationship with God and people. She built her relationship with God by spending time with Him in prayer, and she lived her life in communion with people and God. I came into communion with her and God simply through silently adoring our Lord with her each week.

My experience with Joyce taught me something really important about all relationships. The key to understanding our relationships is to think of them first in the context of God. Our relationships are connected, because we were all made by God, for God, to love and serve God! Therefore, it is critical to recognize that our relationships are the foundation of who we are and of our purpose in life.

Every person we encounter, even in passing, is a relationship. The question is: What is the depth of the relationship, and why has God placed them in our life? Perhaps the only reason they are placed in our life is for us to smile at them and love them for a moment. In Joyce's case, she was placed in my life to teach me how to adore our Lord in silence and lead a life of humility. Only God knows why I was placed in her life.

MAN FULLY ALIVE

During the creation story in Genesis, there's only one time that God says something is "not good." The water, the sky, the light, plants, and animals — all of these were good. Even man was *very* good. But after God created Adam, He said, "It is not good that man should be alone; I will make him a helper fit for him" (Gn 2:18). In all of God's creation, the one thing that wasn't good was that Adam was alone. That's still the same for us today: It is not good for us to be alone. We need other people in our lives.

Because we were made in God's image and likeness, our relationships are meant to imitate the relationships of the three Persons of the Trinity. We see that most clearly reflected in marriage and family. But we can apply the same relational idea to our friendships, our coworkers, and even the brief encounters we have with the many people who move in and out of our lives each day. God, by His very nature, is relationship. He lives in communion. In His relationships with us, God is constantly drawing us closer to himself, helping us to be the best possible version of ourselves — what Saint Irenaeus calls "man fully alive." And if God is all about communion and unity, then the devil is all about disunity and division.

We should be seeking to imitate God in our relationships and have the humility to realize that we can't make it through this life alone. Authentic relationships should be oriented to recognizing the good in others, helping them grow in virtue, and practicing gratitude. Living in isolation is dangerous, because it cuts us off from the people God gave us to help us grow in holiness.

CREATING GOOD RELATIONSHIPS

You have the ability to initiate healthy relationships. However, I should note that this doesn't mean that the other person can or will respond. Still — you have the power to try! It does not matter whether you are an extrovert or introvert, because a relationship should always start with realizing that you and the other person are both children of God.

Recognizing the other person is the start of any good relationship. We need to recognize the importance of the other person and their life journey. This is what made them who they are today and, just like you, it is how they formed their ability to relate to other people. Their story is the reason they respond to you as they do — however that may be. We need empathy to see others for who they are, and to understand where they're coming from.

In order to advance the mission of the Church, we have to build relationships. Good ones. We can start to do this by recognizing that everyone around us has different expectations and limitations based on their own experiences. By walking with other people on their journey, we can invite them into the most important relationship: the relationship with God, who is Father, Son, and Holy Spirit. This begins by introducing them to Jesus. This is what I love about the idea of strengthening relationships as a way to advance the mission. You don't need to be a street corner preacher or travel to foreign lands to bring people to Jesus. It's all about building good relationships with the people already in our lives.

When it comes to building relationships, I think there's a common misperception in our society that a good relationship is one in which there's no conflict. People think that everything's okay as long as it all appears to be going smoothly. After twenty-three years of marriage, I can definitely say that good relationships don't just happen. They take hard work and sacrifice, and conflict with charity is what helps make a relationship healthy! Healthy conflict can and should also exist in all our relationships: in our families, in our friendships, in the workplace, and in our parishes.

I always go back to what Bishop Thomas Olmsted says about friendship: It's about helping people grow in virtue. Sometimes being truly charitable means allowing conflict to exist. It probably doesn't sound like those two words ("friendship" and "conflict") belong in the same sentence. Sometimes, though, conflict is the most loving thing to do. When you have true charity for someone, you want them to be the best version of themselves. That can mean calling them out when they're not being their best self. This is why trust is so important in a relationship. There needs to be an acknowledgment that you have the other person's best interests at heart, and that you are speaking and acting in love when you're pointing out something they are doing that is contrary to showing God's love.

When I think of trust and conflict, I immediately remember my parents. I think I gave my mom plenty of heartburn for the times I disagreed with her. She never initiated conflict with me for the sake of being mean or selfish. It was always to lovingly redirect me to the right path.

As parents, Rosemary and I often need to challenge our daughters when we feel they are straying off the path to holiness. With love, we remind them to ask themselves what God is asking of them. More often than not, this means, at least for the moment, that we are not their favorite people.

Before you can have healthy conflict, there must be established trust in the relationship. This trust will allow both of you to bring the conflict to a resolution. My kids know we want the best for them, just as I knew my mom wanted the best for me. Trust like this allows an openness for dialogue, if conflict is done with love.

In my own life, I've found that the best times for people to challenge me to grow in virtue are when our relationship already has a good foundation of trust. When I know someone truly cares about me, and isn't just trying to hurt me, I am more open to hearing that I did something wrong or hurtful. We never know when we may have to share or receive a difficult truth, so it is imperative for us to build relationships of trust. This can be challenging, but remember — authentic friends help each other grow in virtue.

Modern culture makes this difficult, because it sets the standard that true friendship means supporting people no matter what they do. I couldn't disagree more. Just because we feel or believe something, that doesn't mean it's right. We have to be careful in just following our feelings, as they can mislead us. True friends are there to lovingly guide us back to the right path when we wander. And all of us wander sometimes.

In true Christian friendship, we acknowledge that there is a moral right and wrong and invite each other to live according to that. As a side note: When it comes to morality, I can't express enough how important it is to show Jesus before you preach Him. If people don't experience the love of Jesus in how they interact with you, they won't be open to hearing you talk about Him or His moral teachings.

CHALLENGE

Authentic relationships take work. In order to make them work, we can't stay in what's comfortable. In order to call people on to virtue, we need to be willing to love them by holding them accountable and creating conflict when necessary. Each of us also needs to be open to receiving challenging feedback and correction from the people with whom we are in relationship. We do all this with the end goal of drawing closer to Jesus, together with our loved ones. This is not easy. I invite you to spend some time reflecting on the following questions:

- Within your relationships, do you avoid conflict? Are there relationships in which you are okay with conflict? What are they? What are the relationships where you struggle with conflict?
- Do you spend time intentionally building relationships, or are you content to coast with the relationships you already have? Are any of your relationships in autopilot?
- Some like to argue for the sake of argument. When you speak about moral issues, is it for the sake of the issue or the person? If you asked a friend, how do you think they would answer this question about you?

6
JUST BE KIND

In December 2003, Rosemary and I took our two daughters to see *The Nutcracker*. Abigail, who was just three at the time, was acting up and wouldn't stop crying. Rosemary had been looking forward to taking the girls to the performance. Naturally, she was very frustrated and thought maybe the whole family should just leave. I didn't particularly care for *The Nutcracker*, so I heroically volunteered to take Abby out and wait until it was over.

This left me with about two free hours, which I decided to use to go shopping for Rosemary's Christmas present. Abby and I ended up at a jewelry store in the mall, because that was where I had a credit card. As I was looking at the jewelry, I realized that I recognized the salesman behind the counter. David had been a senior when I was a freshman in high school, and he had been one of the most popular guys in school. He was a star athlete and probably the best-looking guy in school as well. I hadn't seen him in over ten years. I really didn't know David personally, but he might as well have been a celebrity in my town — I mean, he was David!

As David walked over to help me, I was star-struck. He recognized me, too. "Kenny de Leon? Is that you?" ("Kenny" was my nickname growing up.) Now I was even more surprised. David actually knew my name! The most popular guy in school knew who I was a decade later!

I responded, "I don't think I know you ... what's your name?" (I'm a guy, so I had to play it off. Besides, I couldn't let him know how much I'd admired him!)

He said, "I'm David. We went to high school together. I was a senior when you were a freshman. I wouldn't expect you to remember me, since we weren't in the same grade."

"Oh yeah, I think I remember you," I said. "I'm surprised you remember me."

"Of course, I remember you! I could never forget you," he said. Now I was really puzzled. He surely must have got me confused with someone else. David went on, "Back in high school, you did something I'll never forget. Do you remember Alex?"

As soon as he said that, I remembered. Alex was a kid in our school. He had Asperger's and his family struggled financially. As a result, he dressed much differently and stood out from the other students. He was really intelligent, but he always struggled socially. Oftentimes, his clothes were dirty and didn't fit right.

David continued, "One day, I saw Alex walking down the hallway with his pants falling down. He wasn't wearing any underwear and his pants were *really* falling down. Some of the students were laughing at him, and I felt bad for him. Then I saw you pull him aside, take off your belt, and help him put it on. I was blown away. I will never forget that act of kindness."

At this point, I was also blown away. I'd completely forgotten about that day. I remember feeling bad for Alex and wanting to help him. Hearing that story again made me really think about how being kind could make an impact on someone. I also realized: If I did something kind to someone and it was remembered all these years later, then what kind of impact did it have all the times I was not so kind?

I bet most of us have a David and an Alex in our lives. Hopefully, we have shown kindness to many people, and that has made a lasting impact, directly or indirectly. What we do and how we treat people matters. And whether we like it or not, a higher set of standards has been placed on those who identify as a Christian. We represent Jesus to the world, which means our life becomes the witness of what we believe, based on how we treat people.

I believe this is especially true in ministry — whether you are a pastor, deacon, parishioner, or religious staff member, how you treat people matters. People are watching us! Our colleagues, our friends, our families, and our young people are all watching the way we treat people.

This is essential to how we connect with people. We often think building a relationship begins the moment we meet someone with whom we want to have a relationship. In reality, building relationships starts with the way we see people in general and how we treat them.

For example, I always tell my daughters if they want to learn more about a boy they are dating, just watch the way he treats the people around him. How does he treat people at school, his teachers, strangers, servers at a restaurant, or the most vulnerable? On this same note, I remind my daughters that the same rule applies to them.

Even our passing interactions with people matter. Each interaction with another person is providing us with subconscious training, forming the way we think of others. These interactions also reveal whether we truly believe every person is made in the image and likeness of God.

PRACTICING KINDNESS

At the heart of being kind is just one simple thing: remembering that everyone is a child of God. We all are. Each child of God has dignity and value because they are His creation and He loves them. God has given us to each other for a reason. It's important that we recognize this and learn to appreciate people for who they are and the gifts that God has given them. Authentic kindness grows out of that realization that everyone is a son or daughter of God.

Kindness doesn't always come naturally. We should strive to practice kindness, not only with people we know, but also with strangers. It's not complicated, although sometimes it can be challenging. We do this by showing the love of Jesus to everyone, from the server, to the receptionist, to the CEO, to our friends and coworkers. Often we forget that passing relationships are just as important. God may have only put us in someone's life for a few minutes, but that's all we need to be kind! Even one small act of kindness can make a huge impact in someone's life.

It's important to realize, too, that being kind is more than just being friendly. It's coming to an understanding that everyone is on a journey and everyone is in a different place on that journey. We need to choose to love people no matter where they are in their journey.

Kindness is like any other virtue: It's a discipline that we need to practice. Look for opportunities to be kind, not just when it's easy, but also when it is a challenge. Doing that now will make it easier for you to be kind when you really don't want to be. Giving up your seat, opening the door for someone, or smiling and saying good morning are all acts of kindness which help acknowledge that the lives of others matter.

MOVING FROM TRANSACTIONAL TO RELATIONAL

Kindness helps us to move from being transactional to being relational. A transactional mentality is one that's focused on getting the job done. When we have this mentality about other people, we can end up treating them like parts in a machine without meaning to. The impact this has on people we work with or serve in ministry is the opposite of what we are called to believe. The Catholic Church teaches us that every human life is sacred, has dignity, and is the foundation for the moral vision of society. If we look at the work we do and the people we serve as just getting the job done, then we are not living what the Church teaches us.

On the other hand, a relational mentality recognizes that every interaction we have impacts a person, even if it's only for a moment. This is especially true for those of us who work in ministry, whether in a parish, at a diocese, or in some other capacity. Every job we do affects people in a personal and profound way.

One day, I was sitting in a church office waiting for a meeting to start. As I sat there, a young mother came in, holding a baby in a car seat with a toddler in tow. I know from experience how challenging that is to manage! The church secretary acknowledged her and told her she'd be with her in a minute. Several minutes later, the secretary finally asked, "How can I help you?"

The mom asked about how she could get her two kids baptized. The church secretary responded that the baptism coordinator wasn't in. She could leave her contact information, and the coordinator would call her later. During this conversation, I noticed the toddler getting more and more antsy.

The mom said that she had just moved to the area, and the two kids' dad was no longer in the picture. She said, "My parents told me that we really need God in our lives. So, I'm trying to do that and find a job, and I'm kind of overwhelmed." The secretary again directed her to fill out a form for the baptism coordinator, who would call her back later.

Just as the mother appeared ready to leave, the baptism coordinator walked through the front door and headed back to her office. The parish secretary made no attempt to connect her with the woman. But the woman recognized her. She said to the coordinator, "Excuse me, I think I recognize you from the parish website — are you the baptism coordinator?"

The coordinator said, "Yes that's me. Do you need something?"

The young mom went on to retell her story about how she was new to the area, raising two kids by herself, and wanted to bring them into the Faith. She started asking questions about the steps to take to baptize her kids, and it seemed that the coordinator was less than enthusiastic to help her. Clearly frustrated, the mom eventually filled out the form, gave it to the coordinator, and left.

I was disappointed about this whole situation. Here was a young woman returning to the Church for the first time in years. She'd clearly been through a lot and had poured her heart out to these two women. We should have been jumping for joy that she wanted to bring her two kids into the family of God! If the focus had been on building relationships, the secretary and the coordinator would have asked more about her story, welcomed her back, and rolled out the red carpet to be helpful. Yet it seemed that this whole interaction was just "business as usual."

Beyond the question, "How can I help you?" there appeared to be no sincere desire to help this young mother. The church secretary and baptism coordinator were being transactional, not relational. This was a great opportunity to engage with a future parishioner and begin a relationship between this woman and the Church. Both church employees totally missed the opportunity to be relational.

Let's think for a minute about what could have happened

in that situation if both church employees had been relational. What if the secretary had asked the mother about her children, or offered to play with the toddler while she filled out the registration forms? She had a great opportunity to get to know this woman and learn her story. Why was she coming alone to baptize her child? Why had she waited until the older child was a toddler before baptizing him? A few questions — a simple act of kindness — would have shown this woman that her life was important, that she was loved and welcomed into our Catholic family.

How many times have we heard stories of a guest who's visited our parish, only to be told that they're sitting in someone's seat and asked to move? Or how many young parents make the sacrifice to bring their kids to Mass only to be made to feel like an imposition or inconvenience because the kids are noisy? I've even been in parishes where the priest has stopped Mass to tell parents to take their kids out! These might be some extreme examples, but things like this happen often. Each of these situations is really an opportunity for all of us, from parishioners to pastors, to be more relational and kinder to people. It starts with deciding to put people first, and to be relational, not merely transactional, in every interaction.

BEING PRESENT TO ONE ANOTHER

I once asked my pastor in Corpus Christi what the most important part of being a priest was. I expected him to say something like prayer or saying Mass. He didn't. He told me that the most important job of a pastor is to love his people with all his heart. Anyone who knew my pastor knew this was exactly what he did! He loved us by being present and taking an interest in our lives. He asked us how we were doing and made spending time with us a priority.

He knew that being relational required him to be present

in the lives of his people. He knew this would help strengthen his relationship with his flock and allow him to be a witness to Jesus' love for them. He made an effort to show up to parties, sporting events, or school plays. He was active in the community and in the lives of his parishioners. It was not uncommon to run into him at someone's home watching the Dallas Cowboys or San Antonio Spurs game. Through that kindness of just being present, his parishioners knew that he loved them.

I've had some priests tell me that they can't be everywhere for everyone, so they choose to err on the side of caution and not be present at all. They don't want to appear to be playing favorites in the parish, so no one gets any more or any less time with them than another person.

If that's been your approach to ministry, I want to ask you to reconsider and think about Jesus' life and ministry. He didn't go everywhere — He couldn't! He had a small group of close friends, with whom He spent a lot of one-on-one time, but He also followed the Holy Spirit to go where He was needed. It wasn't uncommon to find Him in the homes of sinners, sharing meals with them. Most importantly, Jesus knew He had to smell like His flock (as Pope Francis says) and be present to His people.

My bishop once told me that it is important that a pastor never be afraid to love and enter into a relationship with a family. He explained that by learning to love a few, a pastor can learn to love more and experience the gift of true friendship in a deeper way.

CHALLENGE

When it comes to building relationships, or repairing ones that are broken, the easiest way to start is just to be kind. To that end, I challenge you to reflect on the following points and take action on them:

- When you were a kid, what is the nicest thing that someone did for you? Write them a thank you note and share how that action impacted you. If you can't get hold of them, commit to praying for them over a period of time. Why do you remember that particular act of kindness? How can you replicate that in someone else's life?
- How can you be kinder to the people you work with? Perhaps it could be as simple as saying good morning to everyone when you arrive at the office, or saying goodbye before you leave.
- How often do you hold the door open for someone? How often do you call someone to tell them "good job" or to say "thank you?"

Part III
BOLDLY GROWING ENGAGEMENT

"Trust in the Lord with all your heart,
and do not rely on your own insight.
In all your ways acknowledge him,
and he will make straight your paths."

Proverbs 3:5–6

For many of us who work for the Church, we have a tendency to measure "engagement" merely by how many people are present in the church building for weekend Mass. Although people's physical presence is a good indicator of participation, it is not the only one. Authentic engagement is all about how we show love to people and invite them to live their lives as active disciples.

In order to boldly grow engagement, we must each embrace our role as a missionary disciple. Sometimes we lean on catechesis programs, retreats, formal training, or faith-sharing groups to make disciples. These are certainly good, but on their own, they aren't adequate to truly make disciples.

When I first came into a personal relationship with Jesus, it took me some time to realize that I was a disciple. In my mind, discipleship was for the holy men and women who have been going to church forever. I figured I had to get more education, so I went on to get a master's degree in theology, thinking that would make me a disciple. I was so wrong!

True discipleship does not come with a start or end date, a certificate of completion, or a degree. Discipleship comes from a deep realization that Jesus is Lord, and we want to do everything He says — including loving one another as He has loved us.

This is where the rubber hits the road in discipleship. Having the courage to love, to "will the good of another" (*Catechism of the Catholic Church*, 1766), is not always easy. If it were easy, our Church would look much different. But many times our humanity gets in the way, and we fail to live as engaged disciples.

We cannot worry about rejection or judgment. Instead, we should welcome and encourage people to build their relationship with Christ and His Church. Then we need to begin walking with them, forming them in how to do that. This is exactly what Jesus did with His disciples: He called them, built a relationship with them, and formed them. Boldly growing engagement means taking responsibility to help our brothers and sisters in Christ embrace their relationship with the Church.

7

BE NOT AFRAID: YOU ARE A MISSIONARY

Earlier I spoke about a time in my life when I was waiting on God to show me what He wanted me to do with my life. I did not have a job and was begging God to give me direction. One night, I had a dream where Jesus came to me and told me to go to the bishop of Corpus Christi and say, "Jesus sent me to you, and I'm willing to do whatever you want." I woke up from that dream at 3:00 a.m., super excited and ready to call Bishop Edmond Carmody as soon as the diocesan offices opened. But by the time 8:00 a.m. rolled around, I had lost my nerve. I started second-guessing myself, not willing to believe that God had really spoken to me in a dream, and too afraid to take the leap of faith to make the call. I was sure the bishop would think I was crazy.

I am not the first person to hear a call from God that required a step outside of my comfort zone. The Bible is full of stories of people who heard God ask them to do something. Some responded in faith, like Abraham, who left his homeland with his family and never looked back. Moses did the same thing when he heard God speak in a burning bush. He risked everything to go back to Egypt to speak to Pharaoh. I think that this is the way a relationship with God is. It requires us to leave behind our old lives and step out of our comfort zones to follow Him wherever He leads. So many of us, myself included, are comfortable where we are. Our lives are safe and secure. But in order to be missionaries, we need to put the mission first, and ourselves and our egos second.

In order to boldly grow engagement, we must see ourselves as missionaries, and we must be willing to go out into the unknown and invite others to hear God's voice.

MODERN-DAY MISSIONARIES

When you think of missionaries, what is the first thing that comes to mind? When I first came into a relationship with Jesus, I was excited to evangelize, but still terrified of what God might ask me to do. I was afraid that God would ask me to go live in poverty in some third-world country and preach the Gospel there. Over the years, I have come to realize that we're all called to be missionaries, but for most of us, it doesn't look quite like I imagined. Being a missionary doesn't always mean going to new people in a new land. Instead, it means we must leave our comfort zones to follow what God is asking of us in our ordinary lives. Missionary territory for us may be our families, our offices, our schools, or our parishes. The people we are called to evangelize are right in front of us!

This should challenge us never to be complacent where we are. We may have been an employee, volunteer, or active participant in the Church for years. Still, it is important that we hold ourselves to a high standard of discipling to the people God has put in our path. We can only do this if we recognize that we need one another, and we are compelled to love.

Being a missionary where you are doesn't necessarily make it easier. In fact, I think sometimes it can be harder to share the Gospel with the people already in our lives, for one big reason: We are afraid. Even now, my own fear of rejection or failure often gets in the way of proclaiming the Good News of Jesus to people. It takes a lot of courage to move past that fear and to trust in what God is asking me to do. One of my favorite Scriptures is "Trust in the LORD with all your heart, and do not rely on your own insight. In all your ways acknowledge him, and he will make straight your paths" (Prov 3:5–6). This trust in God is crucial to being bold in proclaiming the Gospel.

Thankfully, when I was too afraid to call the bishop of Corpus Christi like Jesus told me to, that was not the end of the story. A year later, my pastor, Monsignor Morgan, suggested that I apply for a job with the Diocese of Corpus Christi. I'll tell you more about that story later. The end of the interview process was a face-to-face meeting with the bishop. After he offered me a job, I shared with him the dream I'd had a year ago and how I had chickened out and didn't call him. I was still afraid that he'd think I was crazy! He just laughed and said, "Cande! You should have listened to Jesus! You should have called!" If only I had trusted God enough to move past my fear — who knows what would have happened!

TRUST IN THE LORD

We are conditioned as kids to create our own paths. How many times have you heard that you can do whatever you put your mind to? That anything is possible with hard work? Rosemary and I have taught this to our girls, but we have also taught them to seek the will of God and ask Him to direct their paths. Being a disciple of Jesus means following His will for our life and setting our mind to that. The question for us is: How do we find out what God's will is? And, once we do, how do we live it?

To that end, I'd like to offer you three basic principles I've learned over the years for following God's will. Just because I've learned them doesn't mean I've perfected them. Living these out is going to be a lifelong journey for me, as I learn to trust in the Lord with all my heart and allow Him to direct my paths.

Key Principle #1: Ask God to use you.

Very early on in my walk with the Lord, Rosemary told me to ask God to use me. You might remember how I gave Nate the car? That was the fruit of asking God what to do and listening. This is the same idea. If you want to do God's will, you first need to ask Him to use you. This is the first step and shows God that you are open to letting Him work through you. Like me, you might be afraid of how He might answer you. Maybe He's going to ask you to do something that you hate! I don't think He will. But He might ask you to do something that's hard or requires you to step outside your comfort zone. Remember, He created you for a purpose, and His will for you is not going to be contrary to what's already in your heart. The real question is: Have you asked God to use you, and are you willing to respond?

It doesn't matter where you are on your journey with God. His will is always there, no matter if you're just starting out or have been walking with Him for years. He has a plan for everyone at every step of their lives. Your life has a plan and purpose, and God wants to use you as a missionary disciple to bring other people to Him. If you're a priest or work actively in Church ministry, maybe that's easier for you to see. If you're not on the frontlines of ministry, it might be harder. Regardless of the role God has given you in the mission of the Church, you *are* a part of that mission. Your life is a gift, and God wants to use you to bring people to Him. Just allow Him to direct your path.

Key Principle #2: Ask God what He wants you to do.

Asking God what He wants you to do requires humility. It means subjecting yourself to His will and laying aside what you want. When you ask God what He wants you to do, you may not audibly hear His voice, although that does happen sometimes. But He will answer you in other ways. You may hear Him speaking in your heart or through other people. He may just open opportunities or put providential circumstances in your life that lead you to what He wants. He may let you see what He has already put in front of you to do.

God's will is not always found in the big decisions. He often uses the smaller decisions in our lives to guide us to what He wants. When I was unemployed and asking God to tell me what to do, I felt so guilty that we didn't have anything to give back to God. Very soon after this, my pastor asked me to teach a class at the parish on personal finance. I jumped at the chance. I might not have had money to give to God, but I gave back through service. At the end of the class, my pastor offered to pay me for my time. I said no — the class had been meant as a gift to God, and if I received payment, it would not be a gift anymore.

It was hard to turn down payment because I knew our family needed it, but I knew I had to do it. That small decision had long-term consequences. I believe that God used it to open the door for what He ultimately wanted. A year later, because of this encounter, my pastor recommended me for the job I ended up getting with the diocese of Corpus Christi. I was faithful to God in a smaller decision, and He used that to help me follow His will for my life.

Key Principle #3: Be courageous and go!

Sometimes God can ask us to do things that are not easy, like calling up the bishop and telling him God sent me to Him. In that situation, I let fear get in the way of doing God's will. If you're afraid of following what God is telling you to do, I ask you this: What's the worst thing that could happen? Maybe you'll look crazy in front of someone. Maybe you'll be uncomfortable. Maybe you'll fail the first time around.

But what's the best thing that could happen? You'll end up living out the plan that God has for you, which is ultimately the plan that will bring joy and peace to your life and bring others to Jesus.

When I got offered a job in Phoenix, Rosemary and I were both scared. Saying yes meant uprooting our family, leaving behind loved ones, and going to a place where we knew no one. Ultimately, she encouraged me to take the job, because she said it was an answer to that prayer for God to guide me. We couldn't be afraid to follow His guidance. If God is asking you to do something that is scary, I encourage you to not be afraid. Trust in the Lord with all your heart!

CHALLENGE

Take a few minutes and read back through the three key principles for following God's will. If you haven't already, ask God to use you. Ask Him to show you what He wants you to do. Once He shows you, don't be afraid to act! As you read, reflect on the following questions:

- Do you know what God might be asking you to do?
- What is stopping you from being courageous and moving forward?
- How can you apply Proverbs 3:5–6 to your life? Where is God asking you trust Him with all your heart instead of leaning on your own understanding?

8

ENGAGING PEOPLE FOR THE MISSION

Several years before my encounter with the Lord, our family had finally started going to church on a regular basis. Rosemary usually dragged me to church because I didn't want to go. One Sunday morning, we went with our two daughters as usual. At the time, Abby had a doll named Kiki. After we'd left church, fought through the parking lot crowds, loaded the kids in the car, and were driving home, we realized that Kiki wasn't with us.

I wanted to leave her behind and just look for her next week, but Rosemary, knowing how upset Abby would be, insisted that we go back for her. By the time we got back to the church, the parking lot was empty. As I went into the church to look for the doll, a man walked up to me and asked, "Is this yours?" He was holding Kiki.

He introduced himself as Leo. He told me, "I see you here on Sundays with your wife and kids. I just wanted to welcome you to the parish." He then started asking me about my family and our spiritual journey together. I was not really interested in a conversation at the time, so I just said something about how we were trying to go to Mass as often as we could. Leo told me that he had kids too, and he knew it was hard. He encouraged me to keep coming to Mass. As I was trying to leave, he said, "Hey — we have a prayer group here. You should come!" I said "Maybe," but I really meant "No." By that time, we'd talked so long that the lights in the church were turned off.

When I got back to the car with the doll, I told Rosemary about my encounter with Leo. She had been wanting to find a way to connect with the parish community for a while, and she loved the idea of going to a prayer group. I wasn't so on board.

Through this encounter, Leo demonstrated perfectly what boldly growing engagement is all about: being courageous enough to connect with people and to invite them to take the next step in their walk with the Lord, even when they don't seem all that interested. This is what authentic love is: to invite people to participate in the greatest thing ever — a relationship with Christ and His Church. God has put people in our lives for a reason — so that we can share His Good News with them. If we trust in Him, He will take care of us and give us the grace to speak.

BECOMING ENGAGED

It is important to remember, though, that before we can help other people become more fully engaged, we need to first be engaged ourselves. How many times have you heard the line, "You can't give what you don't have"? It's so true — if you don't know Jesus, how can you invite others to know Him? In my story above, Leo was engaged in his faith. I always saw him at Mass, so when he spoke to me, I knew that I could trust him. The only reason that he was able to invite Rosemary and me to grow in our faith was because he had such a strong relationship with Jesus, and he wanted to share that relationship with us.

When Rosemary and I first met, she was Baptist, and she was not afraid to share her faith. When I asked her to marry me, she said no at first, because I didn't know Jesus. She said, "You're Catholic and you don't even know why you believe what you believe!" Eventually, she did agree to marry me, but her conviction in her faith planted a seed of an idea in my heart that maybe there was more to my faith. Still, it took me years to get to a place where I was willing to encounter Jesus. Once I did, I wanted everyone to know Him. I became unafraid, and I would go looking for people who were willing to listen to me share the Gospel. Before my conversion, there was no way I would have been willing to do that!

I think a lot of the time we choose not to share the truth with people because we think it's not our job. Maybe you're not the youth minister, pastor, or RCIA coordinator, but nevertheless, you are a disciple, and therefore you are an ambassador for Christ. It doesn't matter what your job is — you are called to evangelize and make disciples.

I would invite you to spend some time reflecting on how God is specifically calling you to grow engagement. Each of us has different gifts and a different way to answer that call. These things are unique to us. I find that these three points are helpful in guiding that reflection:

1. Ask yourself: What is in your heart? God puts desires and inspiration in our hearts for a reason. That thing that you're passionate about might be the way that He is calling you to engage with others. What do you see that needs to change or that you would

like to impact?

2. Discernment is key. Spend time considering your motivations — why is that desire in your heart? Maybe God wants you to act, or maybe He is trying to show you something about yourself. Invite God to help you make decisions about how to act on what's in your heart.

3. Act with confidence. Your actions might not always be exactly right, but if you followed the first two steps, you can say with a clean conscience that you did not act impulsively. You are doing your best to follow God's voice.

LOS PESCADORES

My encounter with Leo didn't end that day in church. There's actually more to the story, but it's not mine to share — it's Rosemary's. So, I asked her to tell it in her own words:

> The week after Cande had met Leo, we went back to Mass as usual. Leo and his wife, Minnie, came up to us after Mass. Minnie introduced herself to me and said, "Leo said he met Cande last week. I'm so glad to meet you — we've been seeing you and your beautiful family at Mass every week!" She was very loving, gentle, and kind to us. She re-extended her husband's invitation to come to their prayer group and told me she'd love to have us join them.
>
> I talked to Cande about us joining. He still wasn't excited about the idea, but I said yes anyway and committed our family. Although we'd been going to St. Peter's for a couple of years, we really hadn't found a place in the church community. In contrast to the Baptist church I'd been raised in, I found the Catholic Church a little

unwelcoming. After several years of us attending weekly, no one had ever talked to us! Minnie and Leo were
the first, and I felt like this had been what I was waiting
for.

We started going to the prayer group every week,
where we read Scripture and shared our faith and our
lives. We were the youngest couple with the youngest
kids, so for us to have these Catholic role models was
a huge blessing. They really became our family in faith.
Our prayer group had committed to bringing in new
families. That became our mission — so much so that
we decided to name our group "Los Pescadores" (The
Fishermen), after the story in the Bible where Jesus tells
His disciples that they will be fishers of men.

Rosemary and I were about twenty-five years old, had been married for about five years, and she had just become Catholic about
two years before this encounter with Leo and Minnie. I'll save
her story of conversion for another day!

Although this prayer group was what Rosemary had been
waiting for, I was still not an engaged Catholic. Even in that
group, I was just going through the motions and trying to find
my place. This all happened before that night when I encountered Jesus in a personal way. Looking back, I can see that the
level of engagement that the people in this group had with their
faith was slowly creating an openness in my life to hear God's
voice. Through their witness, I was being prepared for my own
encounter.

As a church, we need to find ways to engage people like this:
to help them know that they are part of the community. They are
seen. Your personal witness could be the reason that someone
else will become open to encountering the Lord. As I mentioned
before, the only reason I was at all open to accepting Leo's invita-

tion to the prayer group was that I'd seen him, week in and week out, actively involved at church.

In the last section, I invited you to reflect on how God is calling you to be engaged in your faith. Now I would like to invite you to reflect on *who* God is calling you to engage with. Maybe it's someone you see at church every week, whom you've never met. Maybe it's the barista at the coffee shop you go to every morning. Maybe it's your coworker in the cubicle next to you. Let God show you who He's put in your life and how He wants to use you to invite them to take the next step in their faith journey.

In my own life, this has been difficult sometimes because I don't know what the outcome will be. That's why I always go back to Proverbs 3:5: "Trust in the LORD with all your heart, / and do not rely on your own insight." This reminds me that I'm not the one who makes things happen — God is. Our job is just to extend the invitation to people to come deeper into their walk with Jesus, and we trust in Him to do the rest. I see a lot of other denominations who are on fire to evangelize and invite people to engage with their faith. For some reason, Catholics are often so afraid to do this. This needs to change! I am a disciple and so are you. It's our job to "go … and make disciples" (Mt 28:19).

IN THE CHURCH

For those of us who work or volunteer in the Church, boldly growing engagement can also take a different form, which I think is important to address. Over the years, I've encountered many people in a lot of different ministries who are serving the Church but are not fully engaged with the mission of the Catholic Church.

They're kind of on their own program. This shows up in many different ways in parish life. Sometimes you see it in the person who is not willing to adapt what they're doing in order to best serve the mission of the Catholic Church, because "this is the way we've always done it." Other times you'll see it in the person who may be working or volunteering in the parish, but who is more transactional than relational. Sometimes the person is even bitter and unhappy in their role. Often, they just need to let go of the work they are doing.

These people can seem completely unapproachable. Often others in the parish are afraid to confront them, because they're the only person filling a particular role. If you upset them, you've lost a needed volunteer or employee, or perhaps an argument will arise, and you don't want that confrontation in your life.

If you've met this person, the temptation can be simply to get frustrated with them or talk about how terrible they are in serving the Church, without actually talking *to* them. But I'd like to challenge you: Maybe God has put that person in your path for a reason! Not so you can tell them all about what they're doing wrong, but so that you can have the opportunity to invite them to engage in the mission of the Church in a different way.

Before starting that conversation with them, it's important to make sure you are speaking from a desire for the good of the other person. To that end, it's important to have a relationship with that person. You don't want to just walk up to someone and start telling them what they're doing wrong. Instead, we should try to understand them and why they are responding the way they are in their service within the Church.

Like our earlier reflection on how God is calling us to personally grow engagement, remember: If it's on your heart, there's probably a reason. It's important to take time to discern how to approach these kinds of people in your path, and how to show them God's love.

When you can share with a person that their reactions have a great impact on the people they serve, whether it's in their life, their job, or their ministry, then you create an invitation for them to become a part of the solution.

Remember, relationships are the foundation for advancing the mission, so don't be afraid to try building a relationship with some of the most difficult people you encounter in church ministry. When we ask for God's help and approach someone with humility, genuine love for them, and love for the people we serve, then we can't go wrong.

CHALLENGES

When I was new in my faith, I went on a retreat with my parish. My pastor had recently had heart surgery and was sitting off to the side as we were praying. I felt like God was leading me to go over, lay my hands on him, and pray with him. I hesitated, because I knew everyone in the room would see me if I went over to him. What if he said no? What if I looked stupid? Eventually I made the decision to act, and I went over to him and said, "Father, I feel like God is calling me to lay my hands on you and pray for you. Would you be okay if I did that?" To my shock, he said yes! I would like to challenge you to reflect on how God is calling you to act, by praying with the following questions:

- How engaged are you in your relationship with Jesus? What steps do you need to take to grow in relationship with Him?
- Who is God calling you to boldly engage? Why haven't you followed His call yet?
- Ask God how He wants you to boldly grow engagement.

9

DAMAGED RELATIONSHIPS ARE OPPORTUNITIES

Have you ever wondered what life would be like without original sin? We would all be much happier people! Our lives would be completely ordered. We would all be joyful. There would be peace on earth, and we would have an authentically pure relationship with God. Unfortunately, because of the fall of man and our lack of trust in God, that relationship with God is damaged. That brokenness originated with us. We all know the story: Eve was tempted by the serpent, she disobeyed God, then she encouraged Adam to disobey God, and original sin came into the world.

Sometimes I jokingly remind Rosemary that it was the woman who messed it up for us. She is always quick to reply, "Well maybe if the man was doing his job by protecting his wife, there wouldn't have been a snake in the garden in the first place!" As usual, she's right!

In all seriousness, original sin damaged our relationship with God. If we can't get it right with God, then it is unrealistic for us to think that we will get it right with the other people in our lives. Sin will always cause damage in our relationships. Therefore, our only true opportunity to repair those relationships is through humility, forgiveness, and Jesus.

IT STARTS WITH YOU

It can be easy for us to think that the relationships in our personal lives are separate from our work as disciples, especially when we are professional Church workers. After all, what does my damaged relationship have to do with my ability to bring people to Jesus?

In the Sermon on the Mount, Jesus tells us that our relationships with our brothers and sisters have a direct impact on our relationship with God:

> So if you are offering your gift at the altar, and there remember that your brother has something against you, leave your gift there before the altar and go; first be reconciled to your brother, and then come and offer your gift. Make friends quickly with your accuser, while you are going with him to court, lest your accuser hand you over to the judge, and the judge to the guard, and you be put in prison; truly, I say to you, you will never get out till you have paid the last penny. (Matthew 5:23–26)

We can't effectively bring people to Jesus when we are in prison!

And unforgiveness is a prison — one of our own making. We carry our anger, lack of trust, or resentment into new relationships when we don't forgive others or ourselves. At times, it can seem impossible to forgive. For some of us, it feels easier to bury the situation or the hurt and refuse to acknowledge the pain that we have received or caused.

The reality is that refusing to forgive holds us back from discipleship. If we are holding on to hurt and resentment toward another person, it's going to be next to impossible to share the love of Jesus with others. In order to share the His love, we must be able to admit that Jesus loves everyone, even the person who has caused us pain. The person who hurt us or someone we love is still a child of God and is loved just as much as we are.

There was a time after my conversion when someone hurt a person who was very close to me. For a long time, I was so angry at this person that I wanted them out of my life completely. I remember one time I told this to a priest in confession — how angry I was, how much I didn't want to forgive this person, and how I wanted something bad to happen to them. The priest encouraged me to forgive them. I told him I couldn't and that I didn't want to. For my penance, the priest told me to pray for the desire to desire to forgive this person. Very reluctantly, I did so.

A few months later, the person appeared in one of my dreams and told me how sorry they were for what they'd done. In my dream, I saw how much remorse they had and told them, "I forgive you." When I woke up, the weight of all the anger that I had been carrying around was gone. Through that dream, I had been able to forgive.

It can sometimes be tempting to want to fix everyone else but avoid working on our own damaged relationships. However, we can't invite people to do something that we have not yet done ourselves. It takes courage to look at our own lives and to bring healing to damaged relationships. But in order to boldly grow engagement, we need to have that peace in our own lives. If you had a broken arm, you wouldn't ignore it and hope it goes away on its own. You would go to the doctor, get the bone set, and allow it to heal correctly. We need to do this with our own damaged relationships by taking the first step to healing: forgiveness. We need to forgive in our hearts before anything else. If you're not there yet, do what the priest challenged me to do and pray for a desire to forgive.

Sometimes, you may also need to talk to the person who hurt you, so that you can share honestly about your experience. The hope, in doing this, is that the two of you can grow in understanding of each other. This kind of conflict is the sign of a good relationship. Maybe you're the person who caused the damage in a relationship. If that's the case, you need to own it and humbly ask for forgiveness.

I can struggle with this when Rosemary and I are arguing, and I realize that I'm wrong. Oftentimes, I want to just keep arguing, rather than having the courage to stop, admit my mistake, and ask for forgiveness. It's like it's easier to stay in the hole that I created than to get out! Of course, I eventually come to my senses, admit my mistake, and tell her, "I'm sorry." There is so much healing that can happen just in saying "I'm sorry!" (That's also why confession is so important.)

One time, when I was a kid, I did something really bad. I don't even remember what it was anymore, but I had to go to my mom and ask her forgiveness. I'll never forget — I was terrified to tell her what I did, and even more terrified that she might not forgive me. After I confessed, she hugged me and said, "Mijo, I will always forgive you. You just have to ask." I have always seen my mom in this instance as an image of Jesus when He forgives us. There is nothing we can do or say that He is unwilling to forgive, as long as we have contrition and say we are sorry.

There's one last thing to remember when asking for forgiveness: Sometimes the other person might not be ready to forgive you. Rosemary and I always try to apologize to our daughters right away when we realize we've messed up. Most of the time, they forgive us right away, but not always. We've learned to apologize and let it go until they are ready. That's all we can do to repair the relationship in that moment, and it's important we learn to accept what others are able to give.

DAMAGE FROM OUR EXPECTATIONS

Sometimes, what we expect from the people we love and care about does not match what they can give us on their own. We expect them to understand our needs and to love us exactly the way we want them to. Oftentimes, we fail to recognize that our expectations of people do not take into account their own brokenness.

This is not to say that we shouldn't have expectations of the people we love. For example, my wife expects me to show my love to her and our family, and she's right to do so. Unfortunately, I don't always do a good job of this. Sometimes I work late and forget to call or text during the day. Other times, I am not fully present or listening well, and Rosemary gets frustrated with me because of my lack of attentiveness.

In these cases, it is important that I take ownership of my failure and acknowledge that I have not met some of the basic expectations of a father and husband. Thank God, Rosemary recognizes I am a broken person who has good intentions, and is quick to forgive me!

When people fail to live up to my expectations, I always try to come back to something Bishop Olmsted says: "Assume good intentions." Most of the time, when we hurt someone, we don't intend to do it. It is important we try to think the same way about other people. The reality is that we all have brokenness in our lives. When someone hurts us, it is usually unintentional, but we often receive their action as if it was done maliciously. Bishop Emeritus Edmond Carmody from the Diocese of Corpus Christi used to say, "Never confuse ignorance with maliciousness."

If we were to adopt this attitude, can you imagine how differently we would see the world? Jesus demonstrated this attitude on the cross when He prayed, "Father, forgive them; for they know not what they do" (Lk 23:34). As He was crucified, the King of the Universe asked His Father to forgive His murderers because of their ignorance. Through His death and Resurrection, Jesus took on sin to bring redemption to the world. He restored humanity's broken relationship with God. He forgave us so that we might have eternal life.

This is the ultimate example of how a relationship — one which was damaged by original sin — became an opportunity to be restored. We must ask ourselves, "How do I, like Jesus, take on the damaged relationships in my own life and in the Church and look at them as opportunities for restoration?"

Jesus didn't need to take this first step, but He did — in humility and love for us. He had no expectations from any of us. He loved us in all our brokenness, knowing we could never restore our relationship with Him on our own. He still chose to forgive and heal us. With this example that He set for us, how can we not forgive those in our lives who have failed to live up to our expectations? Is it possible that the people who hurt us most, even though it may have been intentional, acted out of ignorance of their role as a child of God? How can we take our damaged relationships and change them into opportunities to advance the mission of the Church?

RELATIONSHIPS DAMAGED BY PEOPLE WITHIN THE CHURCH

I want to speak specifically to those who are working in Church ministry in some capacity. I'm guessing that most, if not all of you, have met people who have been hurt by someone who works for the Church. Perhaps you inherited or encountered these relationships that were damaged, even if you weren't involved in any way. Oftentimes the Church is cited as the problem, when really it is the person(s) within the Church that caused the pain or hurt.

People can be upset with the Church for many reasons. Perhaps it was a previous pastor, their previous parish, their bishop, or even the pope! Sometimes people are upset with the Church because a relative or friend who is Catholic has misrepresented the Church. In these situations, this is your opportunity to be Jesus to them.

In some cases, the person may be in the wrong, and the Church is in the right. It can be tempting to want to just convince the person to admit they're wrong. In other cases, people within the Church have fallen short and have caused great damage and pain to the individual, and we too can find ourselves becoming angry with the Church. Regardless of the situation, you must remember that God has placed you here to help this person who is hurting restore their relationship with God and the Church.

If you find yourself in this situation, I would suggest practicing these steps:

- **Listen to them.** Let them tell you how they felt wronged and what they perceived in the situation. Often, people just need to be heard.
- **Ask questions to understand what happened and what their experience was.** Engaging with them shows them that you authentically care about them and their story. Remember — you are trying to understand where they're coming from.
- **Remind them who God is.** God is loving and mer-

ciful. For better or for worse, He chose humans to
lead His Church, and we're not perfect.

- **Acknowledge their pain and ask them if they
  would be willing to invite Jesus into that pain.**
  Ask them if you can pray with them right then and
  there.

It can be tempting to want to help resolve a person's hurt immediately, but I've found that most people aren't ready for that,
just like I wasn't ready to forgive the person who had hurt me.
It's also important to remember that we can't resolve their pain
— only they can, with God's help. Consider inviting people to
pray for a desire to be healed and to forgive. Encourage them not
to leave the Church, as many do when they're hurt, but to stay
and make a difference, and help others who have experienced
similar pain.

It can feel like the easier thing to do is to avoid these kinds
of uncomfortable conversations. Even if you haven't experienced
what the other person went through, God can still work through
you. When I find myself having these conversations with people,
I try to remember that God put me in this place at this time, and
that He is the healer, not me. I ask Him as I'm listening, "God,
what do you want me to say? How should I respond? Use me
for Your healing, and let Your words come from my mouth." Remember, we are just there to show God's love by listening and
inviting the person to receive God's love.

CHALLENGE

Ultimately, when we encounter damaged relationships in our
own lives or in our ministry, these are opportunities to share
God's love and to bring healing. We're not the healers, just the
ones who God wants to use to allow Him to restore brokenness.
Before we can be used for this, we need to look at our own lives

and see where there may be damage in need of healing. To do that, reflect on the following questions:

- When you think of damaged relationships in your life, who comes to mind? Is there an opportunity to bring healing to that relationship?
- Have you prayed for the desire to desire to forgive or to seek healing in that relationship? If you haven't, I invite you to start doing that now. Maybe God has given you that desire. If so, I encourage you to take the next step — to forgive or to say you're sorry and, if appropriate, talk to the person.
- Is it difficult for you to admit when you are wrong and to say you're sorry? Why do you think this is the case?

Part IV
CONNECTING PEOPLE TO THE MISSION

"But in your hearts reverence Christ as Lord. Always be prepared to make a defense to any one who calls you to account for the hope that is in you, yet do it with gentleness and reverence."

1 Peter 3:15

If we want to bring people to Jesus, we must proclaim the Gospel. We also need to be able to share our own story.

Storytelling, meeting people where they are, and proclaiming the Gospel are the keys to connecting people to the mission of the Church. The Catholic Church is two thousand years old, and she also carries several thousand years of Jewish culture that preceded her founding by Christ. How do we tell the story of the Church? For many today, it can be very difficult to relate to Scripture without an intentional effort to understand it. Therefore, if we want to build up the Body of Christ and advance the mission of His Church, we must be able to articulate how the Word of God is still relevant in our lives today.

To do this, we first need to know Jesus personally. We must know why He is Lord and how we need Him in our lives. We also need to know our own story and learn how we fit into the Church's story. This forms and equips us to meet others where they are, to authentically listen to their story, and to discern how God may be working in their lives.

For most of us, we won't know the exact moment that we will be called upon to give testimony. It is up to us to be ready and willing to share how God has worked in our lives. This opportunity could come to us in the form of a stranger, but usually it's the relationships in our lives that will present more opportunities to witness. This is why it is so important that we seek to live a life that is consistent with the teachings of the Church, and to see every interaction with another person as an encounter with a child of God.

10
STORYTELLING

One night, as we were sitting around the dinner table with our daughters, my wife started teasing me about how we first started dating. When I met Rosemary, I had just broken up with another girlfriend. The Marine Corps Ball was coming up, and I had bought two tickets so that I could take my now ex-girlfriend with me. I took Rosemary instead. She loves giving me a hard time about the fact that I bought that ticket for another woman. We've told that story more times than I can remember, but this time, my daughters tuned in to the fact that I had been dating someone else right before I met Rosemary. It was like it was the first time they'd heard it.

We've been married for twenty-three years, and as of this writing, our oldest is twenty-two. It seems no matter how many times we tell them stories, they are always learning something new from each retelling. This blows my mind: These people I've known so well for over twenty years still don't know my whole story. It makes me stop and think: How many people are there in my life whose stories I don't fully know? Do I know where they came from, who their families are, what their life journey has been?

Stories are what make people amazing. We each have our own that is unlike anyone else's. Each story is like a beautiful, unique painting; there's not another one like it. For this reason, stories play a vital role in evangelization. They are our gift to other people and a powerful way to engage with them. You might be afraid to evangelize because you don't have a theology degree or all the right answers to the tough questions that people will inevitably ask. Telling your story is different. You don't need the right answers. You just need the courage to share yourself. I guarantee you — it's worth it, because no one can tell your story like you can.

Take a moment and recognize that. You have something of great value to share with people. Your life and your experience can make an impact in people's lives; all you have to do is be willing to share it. You can help teach people valuable lessons you have learned in your life, not by preaching, but simply by sharing your story.

For example, when I first started dating Rosemary, I was venting to her one day about my relationship with my mom and some of the struggles I was having with her. Rosemary listened, and when I finished, she started sharing her story with me. Rosemary didn't have a mom growing up like I did, and she told me how hard it was to see other kids with their moms. School drop-offs, Mother's Day celebrations, major life events — there were so many times where a mother played a central role in the life of her friends. But not hers. I'll never forget what she said to me that day: "If I had a mom, I wouldn't be complaining about her the way you are. Your lack of gratitude for your mom is something you need to work on."

As she shared her story, I realized how much I took for granted my relationship with my mom, and how lucky I really do have it. We may have our struggles, but at the end of the day, I know my mom loves me and is there for me. That is such a gift.

In the same way, your story can have that impact on other people's lives. You just need three things:

- Know your story
- Have the courage to share it
- Be mindful of the time to share

SHARING YOUR STORY

In my life, before I could start sharing my story, I had to reflect on it. I spent a lot of time in prayer thinking through my journey and trying to understand how God was working in my life.

Our story will often be the bridge that connects people to the mission of the Church because it is real, authentic, and sometimes messy. No one can argue with your story because it is your own journey through life.

As Christians, and especially as people who work for the Church, I think sometimes we are afraid to be vulnerable and share our journeys. Telling my story often means talking about times in my life where I was weak, or I failed. It's never easy to admit I was wrong, but I've learned that these are the stories people need to hear. There have been so many times in my own life when I have been built up by other people sharing their struggles and failings. It gives me comfort and hope that I'm not alone. Our stories can have that same power for others.

While it's important to tell your story, I've had to learn the hard way that there's a time and a place for sharing. It's important to be discerning, instead of jumping at any opportunity you can find. Jesus didn't share everything with everyone. Instead, He told parables to a lot of people and only explained the meaning to a few. He picked deliberate times to share His story. We need to be the same way.

Relationship-building should be getting to know someone simply for the purpose of getting to know them. Let the process evolve naturally, instead of diving into sharing your greatest life struggle ten minutes into the first conversation. I've done that, only to realize that the other person was *not* in the right place to listen to me. In that situation, the person was angry at the Church, and listening to me preach did little to help them.

Like the parable of the sower and the seed (cf. Mt 13:3–23), there's a time and place where sharing will be most fruitful. As we're building relationships, we should always be trying to follow the Holy Spirit so that we speak when He leads us to do so, not just when we want to. There's a fine balance between courage and prudence. When in doubt, remember that you can't go wrong with listening.

I want to speak especially here to everyone working in ministry, especially to any priests. I've met a lot of priests who shy away from sharing their stories and lean more on filling the role of a shepherd or a catechist. There's nothing wrong with that, but I challenge you to remember that you are a person, too, just like the people you minister to. They need to see that. As you reflect on your own journey, I invite you to consider sharing parts of your story at appropriate times, maybe in a homily, talk, or small group setting. Catechesis and theology are important, but what people remember most are stories. As you share about your own life, I can promise you that this will have a great impact in helping people in their own faith.

In the past few years, since I've been in Phoenix, I've seen our own bishop do this often. As I have heard him speak over the years, I've noticed him sharing more personal stories and lessons he has learned.

One story he tells has deeply impacted me and others. He talks about his mother who, as a small child, was told by the nuns at her school that any time she walked by the chapel, she should stop in and say, "Hi, Jesus! I love you." They told her that, as she kept visiting Jesus, someday she would hear Him speak to her.

Then one day, shortly after her mother passed away, the Bishop's mom stopped in the chapel as usual, but this time she was quiet. It was at that moment she heard Jesus respond, "I love you." In that moment, she knew that everything would be okay — she had built a personal relationship with Jesus.

This is a perfect example of how our stories should be: a reminder to people that God loves us and that He meets us in our time of need and in our brokenness. The Bishop's story resonates with me in a way that no theological treatise on the love of God ever could. It's simple, it's relatable, and it reminds me of how easy it can be to talk to Jesus. More importantly, it has affected my behavior. I find myself visiting the chapel more frequently, popping in, and saying, "Hi Jesus! I love you."

The key for us as Christians, especially when evangelizing, is not just to share our struggles, but to share them in the context of the cross in our suffering and hope. We are people of hope, and that is exactly what the world needs to hear from us.

KNOW HIS STORY

When I first came into a relationship with Jesus, I thought that good evangelization meant having a great elevator pitch. All I needed was a minute or two of someone's time, and I could sell them Jesus — or so I thought. As I've grown in my faith, I've learned how wrong that was.

Evangelization isn't about memorizing all the right Bible verses or knowing all the right theological answers. At its heart, evangelization is just sharing the story of Jesus and how His story gave your life hope. Before we minister to others, it's important that we've spent time getting to know that story. For me, that involved two things: Scripture and prayer in front of the Blessed Sacrament. I would read the Bible and I would take time to sit in adoration reflecting on Jesus' life and what He went through for me. It's important that we, as Catholics, know the story of His suffering, death, and resurrection.

Knowing God's story helps us to understand our own journey. As I read the Scriptures, I try to keep an awareness of God's presence with me. Often, reading and reflecting on Jesus' life reminds me of times in my own life when I struggled.

I ask Him, "Why did this happen? What was happening in this situation?" Instead of trying to answer those questions for myself, I sit and listen for His answer. I just give Him the opportunity to speak, instead of trying to put the puzzle together on my own. It has been surprising to me to watch Him put the pieces together for me. Slowly I have begun to see all the little ways that God has worked in my life to bring me to where I am. I am so grateful!

As I walk with the Lord, I can't deny that He is working in my life in powerful ways. As His mother, Mary, says, "God has done great things for me!" I didn't end up with a wonderful family, great community, and good job all on my own. Looking back, I see His hand in my life, and I am grateful. This is the story that He has given me to share with others.

DESIRE TO KNOW OTHERS' STORIES

Your story is a gift for others. When you choose to share your life with someone else, you are giving of yourself. That's hard! It takes vulnerability. Sometimes, though, it's just as hard to get to know the stories of those around us.

In order to truly want to know other people's stories, we need to be willing to just receive — to set aside our own egos and to listen, understand, and empathize. We can learn from one another and help each other on the journey if we practice listening to one another. A lot of times, our society can be isolating. So many people around us feel alone, like they have no one to talk to about their problems and worries.

Take a minute to think about the people in your life. Your family. Coworkers. The people you serve. How many of those people can you truly say you know well? Do you know their stories — what their family is like, what their faith experience has been, or what they are struggling with? Oftentimes we think we know people because we spend so much time with them, but there is always more to learn.

When I lived in Texas, my dad and I had an annual tradition the weekend before every Christmas, where we would go out to breakfast and then go Christmas shopping for our wives. Now that I've moved to Arizona, we unfortunately don't get to maintain that tradition anymore. One of our last years shopping together, my dad shared a story with me about his life as a teenager. I'd always thought he'd gone straight to Vietnam after high school. During this conversation, he told me that wasn't the case. He had become a migrant worker at the age of fourteen, went on the road from Texas, and ended up spending a year working near Sacramento before enlisting in the Air Force. He was a kid and traveled across the country with no money, no cell phone, and no car! I was shocked. I asked him, "Dad, how come I didn't know this story?"

His response shocked me even more: "You never asked."

Isn't that the way all our lives are? So many people have stories that they want to share, but they are just waiting for someone to ask. Sometimes if we wait too long, we may miss the opportunity to ask. I often think how many times I wish I could have asked my grandparents more, and now they are gone. Don't be afraid to ask people about their journeys. You don't need to have the right answers. You just need to listen.

CHALLENGE

Earlier, I asked you to think about the people in your life and how well you know them and their stories. Before we move on to the next chapter, I challenge you to write down the names of three people: someone with whom you feel really connected; someone you struggle with; and yourself. Think about their stories and experiences. Can you answer the following questions about them?

- What do they struggle with?
- How did they come into relationship with Jesus?
- What has their life journey looked like?

Start with yourself, because you need to know your own journey first. As you're reflecting on these names, if you don't know the answers to any of these questions, that's okay; that's your next assignment! Spend time with these people to get to know them. Share your own story, and hopefully your vulnerability will open the door to them sharing with you.

11

MEETING PEOPLE WHERE THEY ARE

I have a priest-friend who recently went to visit a family at his parish to invite them to consider giving a large financial gift to their parish. On his way over to their house, he felt guilty because this was the first occasion he'd ever taken the time to visit with them. Now the only reason he was going was because the parish needed their financial support.

He had dinner with them, visited with them, and got to know their family better. During his time with the family, there was laughter, stories, and some emotional moments. The majority of the time was spent getting to know each other, and at some point, the priest found the courage to ask the family for a large sacrificial gift. After the priest left the home, he felt really good about the meeting, but still felt guilty that he had never visited the family until he needed a financial gift for the parish.

Over a week or so after the family prayed about the financial request, they decided to give the priest the gift. They shared with him how much they appreciated his visit, and how grateful they were that he took time to ask them for something so sacrificial face-to-face in their own home.

That momentary discomfort and vulnerability for the priest ended up producing great results and connecting the family to the mission of the Church in a greater way! The guilt he was feeling was real, but he set aside his ego for the mission of the Church and was present to a family.

Connecting people to the mission is all about connecting them to Jesus. The best way to do that is the way Jesus connected himself to us, as Philippians 2:6–8 tells us: "Though he was in the form of God, [Jesus] did not count equality with God a thing to be grasped, but emptied himself, taking the form of a servant, being born in the likeness of men. And being found in human form he humbled himself and became obedient unto death, even death on a cross."

The God who literally created the universe came down to live with us. Jesus, the Word made flesh, did this so that we could identify with Him. God himself walked and talked with us. He faced the exact same things that we did. He didn't let the fact that He was God stand in the way of coming to us in our messy and sinful lives. No matter if you're a priest, youth minister, receptionist, stay-at-home mom, or even a doctor, lawyer, teacher, or plumber, this is your mission, too: to go outside of yourself for the sake of someone else. In order to make disciples, you must do it!

GET TO KNOW THEM

The reality is that not everyone in our lives is in a great place. There may be people in your life who are broken or angry. They may be resistant to hearing the Gospel proclaimed. In fact, in my experience, it's rare that someone is immediately ready to hear about Jesus. More often than not, you have to earn that opportunity by getting to know them and what they're going through. The key to this is that you genuinely and authentically want to know them. The world is so busy that many times people don't feel like they're heard. Just spending time with others tells them: Your life matters! You matter!

Sometimes I struggle with the belief that, because I haven't been through what someone else has been through, I can't meet them where they are. Jesus shows us that this isn't true! He never sinned, yet He was able to connect with some of the worst sinners of His day. Scripture is full of stories about Him hanging out with tax collectors and sinners. It didn't matter that He hadn't lived their sin. He was present anyway, and through that, He was able to lead them to an encounter with the Father. Sometimes we don't know what to say or what to do in response to people's brokenness. That's okay. The most important thing is to be present and to love them, no matter what.

When I worked in Texas, the bishop sent me to visit with the warden of one of our prisons. While I was there, the warden took me on a behind-the-scenes tour of the prison. As part of the tour, we went to visit a church music group that was practicing. I was blown away by their beautiful voices. I didn't think I had anything to talk to them about, because I had no idea what they were going through. I didn't know why they were there or what their experience was like being in prison. It was just me and the warden in a room with two dozen men who looked like they could squish me — and I'm not a tiny guy! When they finished singing, the men asked me to lead them in prayer. They were just grateful that I was there. Even though I felt like I had nothing to offer them, I was present, and that was enough for them.

SMELL OF THE SHEEP

In his apostolic exhortation *The Joy of the Gospel*, Pope Francis reminds us that all of us are called to be missionary disciples. The Church is meant to be a community of people that meet people where they are in their journey and take the first step to bring them to Jesus. In Pope Francis's words:

> An evangelizing community gets involved by word and deed in people's daily lives; it bridges distances, it is willing to abase itself if necessary, and it embraces human life, touching the suffering flesh of Christ in others. Evangelizers thus take on the "smell of the sheep" and the sheep are willing to hear their voice. An evangelizing community is also supportive, standing by people at every step of the way, no matter how difficult or lengthy this may prove to be. (24)

The reference the Holy Father makes to the "smell of the sheep" is such a great, tangible example. Take a moment to think about this. Shepherds spend so much time with their sheep that they start to smell like them, and as a result the sheep listen and follow them.

As Christians, this is what it should be like when we reach out to the people in our lives: We need to be dedicated to spending time with them and living our lives with them. We need to show them that we are willing to walk by their side, and we genuinely care for them. Unfortunately, this is easier said than done, and can be a challenge to us. It can be uncomfortable, and may even feel as if it is consuming our time and energy. However, if we are willing to walk with other people and "smell of the sheep," we will gain credibility, empathy, and trust.

When I was in the Marine Corps, we were in Twenty-Nine Palms, California, living out in the field during the summertime.

Spending so much time in the desert terrain, outside in 122-degree heat, our sweat evaporated so fast that our shirts never got wet, and you could see the salt stains left behind. Our entire unit, 5th Marines, had been out there for about forty days, and most of the supplies we took were running low — including our cigarettes.

One day, as we were working, our Sergeant Major came up in a Humvee. He stopped and talked with us and asked us if we had any cigarettes. We said no — we'd run out. He took a carton of cigarettes (ten packs of smokes) out of the car and gave them to us and told us to keep a pack each and share the rest with our friends. We were blown away that he related enough to us that he knew we needed our cigarettes.

As our Sergeant Major, he had every right to stay sitting in the air-conditioned offices rather than joining us out in the sun. Instead, he was out mingling with his men. He was "living with the smell of the sheep," and he earned our respect. I am confident that any one of us would have taken a bullet for him, and we would gladly do anything he asked of us.

When I worked in the Diocese of Corpus Christi, we spent months planning and preparing for a huge diocesan celebration with more than 10,000 people. Just before the event, the planning committee ended up working until after midnight every night for a few weeks, preparing. Our Vicar General spent every one of those late nights with us. Oftentimes, there wasn't much that he could do to help us, but it didn't matter. He was there with his people, enduring the long hours with us. He's now Bishop Kihneman of Biloxi, Mississippi. He smelled like the sheep.

I think the most obvious place to practice this kind of relationship-building is within our families. These are literally the people you live with. Our home is where we do life with people, meet them where they are, and love them day in and day out, no matter what. We can't go out to strangers until we're doing this.

It can also be a temptation to think that, in order to meet people where they are, love them, and share the Gospel with them, we need to be out looking for them. Maybe some people have a calling to do that, but for most of us, God puts people in our lives who need our love. The people we're meant to walk with are often simply our coworkers, friends, and family. I encourage you to reflect on those relationships and ask God who He might be calling you to accompany.

RELATIONAL NOT TRANSACTIONAL

We've talked a bit about how we should seek to be relational rather than transactional, but it's such an important topic that I want to revisit it.

When we're trying to meet people where they are, it's important to do this from a place of love. We're not trying to put in enough time with them to earn a right to preach. The goal is to authentically care about the person God has put in front of you and to try to love them as best you can. It's all about relationship, and we need to be on our guard against any type of transactional mentality that tries to creep in.

When one of my daughters was in fourth grade, she came to me for help with her math homework. I thought to myself, I have a bachelor's degree, a master's degree, and am halfway through another master's degree. This should be easy! But — as any parents who have tried to help with homework know — it wasn't. Half an hour into our time together, we started to argue about the right way to do a particular problem. It ended in her crying and running to Rosemary for help, with me yelling at her to stop crying. I felt like a horrible father because I couldn't teach her simple math. More importantly, I couldn't meet my own daughter where she was.

My problem was that I was being transactional. I was just trying to get the work done instead of focusing on my daughter.

I wasn't trying to get on her level and be with her.

Being relational doesn't always come easily to us. In fact, we can be very transactional in the things that matter most — like spending time with our family, listening to our spouse, or (as in my case) teaching our children. If you find yourself struggling with being relational at times that matter the most, it's okay; you are not alone. Try to be aware of those times when you're focusing on getting the job done, rather than paying attention to the person in front of you. Then acknowledge that you could be less transactional, and work toward being more relational. We have to invite God into every interaction and ask Him for help in being more relational. Maybe it won't happen overnight, but if we persevere and keep asking God for help, we will see ourselves beginning to change in the way we interact with others.

We have to try to live in the present moment and see every interaction with people, in even the simplest of tasks, as an opportunity to be intentional about building a relationship. If this sounds tough — you are right, it is! It takes practice, but it all starts with a desire to be relational.

Jesus was the model for being relational. Jesus never just went through the motions with people. He was always present to people — and He still is.

GOD FIRST

One major challenge many of us face in seeking to meet people where they are is that we haven't experienced this ourselves, so we have a hard time doing it. Maybe no one has ever bothered to meet you where you are. If this is something you struggle with, remember that this is the way God always interacts with each of us. The *Catechism of the Catholic Church* tells us that "at every time and in every place, God draws close to man" (1). He took the first step and came to us and is always trying to meet us where we are.

When I think about this, the place where I experience this most profoundly is in the Sacrament of Confession. Through the priest, God comes right into our messy and sinful lives. He gives us the opportunity to get everything off our chest and then loves and forgives us. All we have to do is receive it!

There are so many times throughout our lives where God is trying to meet us — literally every minute of every day. In the midst of our struggles, sometimes we just need to stop and ask Him how He is trying to encounter us in the midst of our messiness.

Let's turn again to Philippians 2: "[T]hough he was in the form of God, [Jesus] did not count equality with God a thing to be grasped, but emptied himself, taking the form of a servant, being born in the likeness of men. And being found in human form he humbled himself and became obedient unto death, even death on a cross." What Jesus did for us was not nice and neat. Think about it: Jesus became man, took the form of a slave, and suffered and died for us! If we're going to imitate Him, we need to not be afraid of the messy people in our lives. Don't be afraid to just be present to them, walk with them, and love them in the midst of their messiness. You might not always say or do the right thing, but the most important thing is just to love them.

CHALLENGE

This one is simple — just take some time to reflect on the following questions:

- What was a time in your life when someone met you at your most vulnerable?
- What did they say or do, and how did that impact you?
- Do you smell like the sheep? Would the people you work with agree with your answer?

12
PROCLAIMING THE GOSPEL

Shortly after I moved to Phoenix, I had to rent a car for a business trip. At the rental counter, I met Miguel. He was young, charismatic, and energetic. I remember immediately thinking it would be great to work with him someday, so we ended up exchanging phone numbers. A few months later, a position opened up in my department, and I thought of Miguel. I texted him and asked him to lunch, saying that I had something I wanted to share with him.

While I was sitting in the restaurant waiting for him, a man walked up to me and greeted me. I vaguely remembered meeting him somewhere. When he sat down at the table, I realized — his name was also Miguel. I had texted the wrong Miguel! The Miguel I texted was also someone I had met about a year prior, and now I was in a mess because I invited the wrong person to lunch. I learned two lessons here: Call instead of text for invites, and put people's last names and notes in your contacts.

What was supposed to be an intentional moment to recruit someone to my team had just become really awkward. Miguel even told me that he had been surprised to hear from me and that he was looking forward to whatever I had to share with him. I was too embarrassed to admit my mistake, so I went along with it. I told him I had just wanted to get to know him better. A few minutes into the conversation, it was clear that we had nothing in common, and it was obvious that something was a bit "off" about our lunch meeting. I wonder if he knew I had reached out to him by mistake.

After the longest forty-minute lunch of my life, our check finally came, and I offered to pay. "You can just get the bill next time," I said. Miguel looked at me and said, "I think it's pretty apparent there won't be a next time. Let's just split it." Even though he was right, I was annoyed and finally agreed to split the check. As he was getting up to leave, he asked, "What makes you love your job so much that you would move your wife and kids across the country for it?"

I shared with him that I see my work as a ministry. While I have a boss whom I report to, I ultimately see Jesus as my boss. He's in charge and I love having the opportunity to serve Him. I told him that I loved my job because I love my faith. Then I asked him if he was engaged with his faith.

He sat back down, and we started talking more about his journey. He said that he and his wife were thinking about baptizing their two children, but he also shared he wasn't baptized himself.

I asked him why he was thinking about baptizing his kids into a faith that he wasn't a part of. He then went on to share that his parents never took him to church as a child. They wanted him to be free to choose whatever faith he wanted. "I thought it was freedom at the time," he said, "but now I realize that it actually imprisoned me. I feel unable to make a decision now that I can." He said he and his wife had been to multiple churches and tried a lot of different religions, but never found one that resonated with them. He wanted his children to have the opportunity to grow up in a faith. He wasn't sure where to go, but he just felt like baptism was the right decision.

From our conversation, I was pretty sure that he was open to hearing about my journey, so I started sharing with him what Jesus meant to me. I told him my story, and how I came to be in a personal relationship with Jesus. Ninety minutes later, we were still talking. I eventually told him, "I don't think this lunch was a coincidence. God sent me into your life to invite you to consider baptism, not just for your kids, but for yourself. If you want, I will walk with you through that journey."

We met up a few more times after that. I took him to a church and introduced him to some priest-friends of mine. He and his wife eventually ended up becoming Methodist and having their children baptized. While I would have been thrilled if he had become Catholic, I still view this as a clear sign of God's grace at work. And to be honest, it also keeps me humble. Maybe he didn't choose to become Catholic because someone in the Methodist church did a better job of explaining their faith! I praise God that he found a Christian church, and I can only hope and pray that he and his family will one day come to realize the beauty and richness of the Catholic Church that was founded by Jesus.

GOD WANTS TO USE YOU

I share this story with you, because I think it's a great example of how God can work through us to share the Good News with people, even when we least expect it. Let's walk through that.

Divine Appointments

Most of us will never preach from a pulpit or speak in front of large crowds of people. For most of us, our opportunities to share Jesus will come in the form of divine appointments — people God brings into our lives so that we can share our stories with them and invite them into a relationship with Him. When this happens, we can feel a lot of pressure to get everything right, because we think there's no room for mistakes. We absolutely have a responsibility in those moments to be prepared. But I would also caution you not to put so much pressure on yourself.

Most of the time, these moments come up when we're least expecting them, like at the end of that really awkward lunch I had with Miguel. As much as I sometimes wish He did, God doesn't usually show us His plans. We just have to be ready whenever He wants to use us. We need to "always be prepared to make a defense to any one who calls you to account for the hope that is in you" (1 Pt 3:15). We've already talked about an important way to be prepared: by knowing your own story. If you can articulate how God has worked in your life and why you've chosen to follow Him, you're prepared!

Know the Church's Story

Knowing your own story is so important, but we also need to be able to convey the basic Gospel message. This is how I like to tell it:

- Humanity was created to be in relationship with God.
- Sin destroyed that relationship and disconnected us from God. Sin affects our lives and causes brokenness. We're all broken and all experience suffering.
- Jesus came to earth to mend our broken relationship with God by suffering, dying, and rising from

the dead.
- Everyone is invited to accept Jesus' saving work and enter into relationship with God.

This isn't a meaningless story. We also need to be able to share how the story of the Church influences our own lives and how it can impact the person you're speaking to. Think of it like this: As you share your story, you're also sharing how the life, death, and Resurrection of Jesus transformed your life, and telling them that Jesus can do the same for them.

Be Bold

It's really rare that someone will walk up to you and say, "Will you share your story with me? Why is your faith important to you?" I wish it was that easy! Instead, we need to be looking for opportunities to share and be bold enough to speak when they come. When Miguel told me that he wanted to baptize his kids, I could have just said, "Cool. Good for you, man! That's great!" and left it at that. But I saw an opportunity to ask him about his faith journey and, later on, an opportunity to share about my own. I could see that he was open, and even though I knew the lunch was a disaster, I took the chance to share. Being bold means putting our ego last.

Obstacles Are Opportunities

When you come to difficult moments in your life or encounter difficult people, ask yourself: Where is God in this? What is He trying to do? Just like that incredibly awkward lunch with Miguel, God was right in the middle of that discomfort. It can be hard to see sometimes, but I believe that God is always working, especially in difficulty. We just have to have the eyes of faith to see it.

PRACTICAL ADVICE

I saved this chapter for the very end on purpose. For most of us, our opportunities to share the Gospel will come in our daily interactions with family, friends, coworkers, or random chance encounters. That's why building relationships with the people around you is so key. It's through these relationships that you'll have the opportunity to proclaim the Gospel. I want to challenge you to keep your eyes and ears open for these opportunities. I can guarantee that they will be unannounced and unexpected.

It's totally normal to be afraid when these moments come up. With that said, I think this is why it's important to know your story. When you share how God has worked in your life, you are telling a story that you know personally, and so you can't help but have some confidence. Sharing your journey should be natural and shouldn't be uncomfortable. You own it, and it can't be debated.

When we really want to help someone or lead them to something good, we speak with authority. "You have to see this great movie!" "This car is awesome!" "I love her so much — she is the most beautiful woman I have ever seen!" (speaking about Rosemary). My point is that we have confidence, joy, and enthusiasm when we want to share good news! So why not think about sharing the Good News of Jesus Christ with that same zeal? If you're struggling with how to do this, then perhaps think about how Jesus has saved you. Where would you be without Him? Tell your story like your life was saved, because it has been!

I usually get the most nervous when I am speaking about Church teaching or liturgical questions, outside of how God has worked in my life to bring me into His Church. If I am speaking about the Church, aside from my story, I worry what will happen if my listeners ask me a question and I don't know the answer. What if they quote some Church document that I am unaware of? What if they ask me a theological question? I never know how the other person is going to respond. They might think I'm foolish, naïve, or just not very smart.

All of these questions and thoughts are normal — but they also come from our ego. When we are connecting people to the mission by proclaiming the Gospel, there is no room for our ego. The Gospel is not about the way we feel; it is about what Jesus has done for humanity.

Your story is the bridge between the Gospel and the person with whom you are sharing. The Holy Spirit will give you the words that you need! Just remember what Jesus told His disciples: "Do not be anxious beforehand about what you are to say; but say whatever is given you in that hour, for it is not you who speak, but the Holy Spirit" (Mk 13:11).

PROCLAIMING THE GOSPEL

While writing this, I tried to think of people with whom I have shared the Gospel, whose lives I know have truly been impacted. I couldn't think of one person. That doesn't mean I haven't impacted someone's life, but at the end of the day, I just don't know.

What I do know is I have done my absolute best to proclaim the Gospel to my four daughters. For as long as I can remember, Rosemary and I have taught them about the life of Jesus. When the kids were young, we made it a point to teach them that God became man and died for our sins so that we could have eternal life.

We haven't always had the answers to questions our daughters have asked, and we haven't always been a good example. I certainly lost my temper and patience many times. I also failed to lead my family in prayer together or take my family to Mass many times, even though I still tried. It takes time and intentional work to be a better example — especially to your family members, because they know all your vulnerabilities.

With that said, I believe Rosemary and I proclaiming the

Gospel has and will continue to be impactful in our kids' lives. Even when we messed up, our daughters still saw us trying to live the Gospel. They saw the way my wife and I loved and treated each other; they knew we loved them very much; they knew that my wife and I believed in what we were saying to them about faith; and although we were far from perfect, they knew we tried to live what we were saying.

As the kids have gotten older, Rosemary and I have reinforced our teaching about Jesus by telling them how He has changed our lives. In many cases, the kids have witnessed firsthand how Jesus has changed our lives. My hope is that when I die, I will have peace knowing that I did my best to share with my kids all that Jesus has commanded me (cf. Mt 28:20).

This should be the first priority for each of us: How have we shared Jesus with the people who are closest to us?

Our encounters with the people closest to us should always be strengthening a relationship of trust. If we want our words to be well received, we need first of all to think about how we live our lives, and whether we're living in a way that is worthy of the trust of the people in our lives. I think of Jesus when He said: "If I am not doing the works of my Father, then do not believe me; but if I do them, even though you do not believe me, believe the works, that you may know and understand that the Father is in me and I am in the Father" (Jn 10:37–38). If Rosemary and I had not built a relationship of trust and love with our kids, I'm not sure they would accept the Gospel — at least not from us. This rationale applies not just to our families, but to everyone we know. Can the people in our lives receive the proclamation of the Gospel from us?

In a world where we have to be on guard and doubtful of things that are "too good to be true," the Gospel can sound pretty contrary to our common sense. The Good News of our salvation seems infinitely too good to be true — yet it is absolutely true.

As Saint Paul says, "For the word of the cross is folly to those who are perishing, but to us who are being saved it is the power of God" (1 Cor 1:18).

Therefore, we have to live the Gospel before we can share it. Most individuals simply are not ready to accept the Good News the first time they hear it, but they'll be more likely to believe it if they see us living it. It's so important that our actions reflect what we're speaking. This builds credibility for when we do share the Gospel.

People want to know what makes our lives so different. They want to know why we have so much joy, peace, and love for others. In the Gospel of Matthew, Jesus tells us, "You are the light of the world" (5:14). He is right, our faith can't be hidden! Simply by living out our faith, we shine forth God's light in the world, and people will be drawn to that light. Rosemary reminds me the light is not us — it's Jesus, and people want Jesus!

Later on, in Matthew, Jesus says, "Thus you will know them by their fruits" (7:20). What kind of fruit do we produce? Fruits of gratitude, kindness, gentleness, trust, and friendship? Or fruits of gossip, complaining, brashness, greed, and anger? Remember, our fruits are what will lead people to trust us — or not — and they lay the groundwork for proclaiming the Gospel.

CHALLENGE

How do you respond when people ask, "Why do you believe what you believe? Why are you a Catholic?" This is my challenge to you: Can you explain the story of the Church so simply that even a fifth grader can understand it? If you can't, practice! Write it out if you must, and tell the story to a friend until you've got it down. This way, you will "always be prepared to make a defense to any one who calls you to account for the hope that is in you" (1 Pt 3:15).

CONCLUSION

In order to advance Jesus' mission and fulfill our God-given duty to "go and make disciples," we must learn to journey with the people in our lives, to strengthen relationships, boldly grow engagement, and connect people to the mission. These transformational life principles are not complicated, but I can tell you from years of experience that just because they are simple does not mean they are easy to live.

It's not always easy to truly love the person in front of us. It's not easy to walk with someone through the messiness of their lives. I encourage you not to let that overwhelm you. Remember, you were made for this. If God is calling you to be part of His mission, (and since you're baptized, you can be assured that He is) He will help you. You don't have to be perfect — no one is, and I know I'm definitely not! All you have to do is try and, when you mess up, try to do better tomorrow.

If you're not sure where to begin with all this, I would invite you to spend some time in prayer, ideally in front of the Blessed Sacrament — there is really no better place! Ask God to lead you. Ask Him to show you where He wants you to begin, or to show you which people in your life He wants you to connect with. Sit and listen, and then go and do what He says.

A priest friend of mine has made a daily habit of this practice. Every day, he prays that God will prepare him for the people that he is going to encounter that day. He prays by name for the people he knows he'll see — his staff members, the people he has meetings scheduled with, etc. Then he asks God for the grace and wisdom to be present to all the unexpected people he'll encounter that day. Just like this priest, each of us need to ask God for His guidance throughout the day, especially as we encounter others. I bet you'll be surprised by what He does in and through you!

Above all, remember: Advancing the mission of the Church must start with you. And this means it starts with your own life of faith and commitment to Jesus Christ. If you don't have a personal relationship with Jesus, how can you invite others to do the same? So often, it's the way we live our lives that is the most powerful witness of all. People don't always want to listen to what we have to say, but they can't help but notice how we live our lives. Just like we make time in our lives for our spouse, family members, and friends, we must make time for personal prayer with God. If this is not a priority, we simply won't be able to live our call to be part of the mission. The more we make time for prayer and developing a personal relationship with Jesus, the more we will truly be able to evangelize and make disciples.

I want to leave you with one final thought: God has chosen *you*. Your life matters; you have a purpose; you are a child of God, and He loves you. Only you can fulfill the specific mission God has set before you. God has placed that consuming dream or idea in your heart for His glory. People are counting on you to become the person God has created you to be, but only you can take that first step. God is inviting you to be in relationship with Him and a part of His Church. Don't let yourself think that you don't matter — you do! God has called you to be a part of His family and His mission, and He has given you a unique set of gifts and talents to accomplish that mission. You can do this, so, "go forth and make disciples!"

ACKNOWLEDGMENTS

I have come to learn that everything in my life is an opportunity to practice gratitude, to give thanks to God, the source of everything. It is with this in mind that I want to tell you that what I am sharing with you in this book does not come entirely from me. I have learned from the people in my life who have taught me through their generosity, wisdom, and witness.

I have the great privilege of serving Bishop Thomas Olmsted in the Diocese of Phoenix. He has shown me what a saintly man looks like and how to lead with humility. I have also learned a great deal from Bishop Eduardo Nevares, Father Fred Adamson, and Father Greg Schlarb here in the Diocese of Phoenix. Their passion for serving Our Lord is infectious, and they have personally helped my family and me on our journey here. They continually remind me of the importance of relationships, mission, and striving for holiness. Each has helped me become the best version of myself. They practice the principle of gratitude and teach me daily by the way they serve. These priests have helped me professionally in a life-changing way. I am thankful to them and to God forever.

The principles in this book have always been at the heart of the ministry in which God has placed me throughout my life. My two colleagues, Linda Barkyoumb and Lisa Wentz, have really helped me unpackage them through our work, prayer, and discussion together. Linda and Lisa are some of the best in their field and I am grateful to God that He placed them in my life. I am also grateful to work alongside Christina Gavin and the rest of the Office of Mission Advancement. They inspire me every day! Thank you, Therese Beigel, my Executive Assistant, for helping me think through many of my ideas (including this book), and for giving your gifts to help our team in ministry — you are a Godsend.

I would also like to express gratitude for the many people who helped and guided me in Corpus Christi. Bishop Emeritus Edmond Carmody offered me a position in the Diocese of Corpus Christi. Shortly afterwards, Bishop Michael Mulvey gave me the opportunity to share the Spirituality of Stewardship through fundraising and development. I am grateful to both of them for giving me a chance. Monsignor Louis Kihneman (now Bishop Kihneman of the Diocese of Biloxi) was an important mentor and priest who helped me along the way. Thank you for your prayers, counsel, and your continued friendship.

I am grateful for all the priests, religious, deacons and their wives, and the many lay people who God has put in my path: Father Bob Dunn, Father Andrew Kemberling, and Mila Glodova who taught me the Spirituality of Stewardship; Dan Rogers with Revive and my colleagues in Stewardship, Development and Advancement across the country (shout out to Region X); the hundreds of volunteers and colleagues who have helped move the mission forward with me; Sharon Kaiser and all the team at OSV, including the publishing team, I am so grateful for each one of you. Thank you.

Three priests who helped me in the most critical part of my journey, when I first came into a personal relationship with God, were: Monsignor Morgan Rowsome, Father Ralph Jones, and Monsignor Seamus McGowan. These three priests profoundly impacted me in my personal walk with the Lord and how I serve our Catholic Church. I am eternally grateful.

I am grateful to Becky and Rudy Castillo for sacrificing to embrace my wife, Rosemary, as their daughter. They have been terrific parents to Rosemary and me, and special grandparents to our kids. I am thankful to God for the entire Castillo and Mireles family for loving my wife and my family — thank you. My Tio, Angel Leos helped give me direction and taught me about Jesus. Thank you.

I am grateful for the sacrifices and lessons I learned from my mom and dad, Diane and Cande. I inherited my work ethic from my dad, who worked tirelessly six days a week from the moment he woke until he slept to provide for our family. He also taught me the importance of people in our lives. My mom taught our family boldness and gave us the confidence we would need to navigate this world. My two sisters, Deborah and Kelly, have shown me how trust in the Lord, forgiveness, and embracing suffering can be a pathway to peace and holiness. I am truly grateful for both of them and their families.

"Thank you" will never be enough to Rosemary for being my best friend in this journey and my soulmate. I am grateful for the years of encouragement to write this book, and the many hours you spent helping me think it through. You helped me realize that a personal relationship with Jesus is possible. Through you, I learned in a more profound way about practicing gratitude, generosity, empathy, gentleness, and humility. You changed my life forever, and if it was not for you, I am certain I would never have had the opportunity to serve the Lord in this way. Most importantly, you gave me the four greatest gifts of all: Isabella, Abigail, Alexandra, and Sophia. Each day these four young ladies remind me of God's immense love for us — they teach me how to be a disciple.

To everyone else in my life that I did not mention, please know I am grateful to God for you. Many of you helped teach me lessons that formed my perspective and passions. Thank you for being in my life. Your life matters, you have a purpose, you are a child of God, and He loves you. Thank you for being you!

ABOUT THE AUTHOR

Cande de Leon will often say that he is a husband and father first. He has been married to Rosemary for twenty-three years, and they have four children. They currently live in Phoenix, Arizona. For the last fourteen years, Cande has served in diocesan roles leading capital campaigns, annual appeals, and parish offertory enhancement programs. Cande's leadership has helped parishes develop a renewed zeal for evangelization and discipleship while raising over two hundred million dollars to support the Church. Before working in ministry, Cande served in the United States Marine Corps. He then went on to work in his family business, while earning a BBA from Texas A&M Corpus Christi and an MA in Theology from Holy Apostles Seminary and College. He is currently pursuing his MBA. His message is consistent: You are a child of God; your life has value; your life has purpose; and people are counting on you to make a difference.